EDGE COMPUTING IN LOGISTICS

EDGE COMPUTING IN LOGISTICS
Case Studies and Applications

Bo Li

1st Edition
Copyright © 2024 Bo Li
Independently Published.

All rights reserved. No parts of this book may be copied, distributed, or published in any form without permission from the publisher.

ISBN: 979-8-3360-5027-1

DEDICATION

This book is dedicated to my mother, my father, my wife, and my daughter.

NOTES: This book is a refinement and expansion of my previous book on edge computing and supply chain management. I have also added case studies to strengthen the point that edge computing can indeed be applied in logistics applications.

TABLE OF CONTENTS

Introduction 1
    Basic concepts of logistics 1
    Definition and overview of edge computing ... 4
    Edge computing in logistics 10
The Edge Computing Technology 15
    Fundamental principles of edge computing ... 15
    Edge devices and architecture 20
        Edge devices 21
        Edge gateways 22
        Network infrastructure and models 23
        Integration with cloud computing 24
    Edge computing and cloud computing 27
        Differences in architecture and data processing 27
        Data management and bandwidth efficiency 29
        Connections and complementarity 30
Data Processing in Logistics 35
    Data collection 35
    Real-time data analytics and execution 40
    Privacy protection and data security 45
Applications of Edge Computing in Logistics 55
    Coordination with Supply Source 56
        Case study of Grupo Pinsa 57
    Digital Infrastructure 58
        Case study of Gecko 58
    Process optimization 60
        Case study of Tyson Foods 61

- Warehousing and inventory tracking 62
  - Case study of Wendy's 65
- Logistics and transportation optimization 66
  - Case studies of FedEx and Kargo 69
- Delivery to stores and homes 70
  - Case studies of Sensormatic and IBM ... 71
- Autonomous vehicle 72

Emerging Logistics Technologies and Edge Computing 83
- Internet of Things (IoT) and edge computing 83
- Robotics technology and edge computing 88
  - Case Study: Autonomous Mobile Robots for Industry 4.0 Warehouses 90
- Generative AI and edge computing 94

Challenges and Future Trends 104
- Challenges of implementing edge computing in logistics 104
- Future trends and technological outlook 108

Conclusion 113

INTRODUCTION

We shall introduce the logistics and edge computing concepts in this chapter.

Basic concepts of logistics

Logistics is a critical component of supply chain management, encompassing the planning, implementation, and control of the efficient movement and storage of goods, services, and information from the point of origin to the point of consumption. It involves various activities, including transportation, warehousing, inventory management, order fulfillment, and packaging. The primary goal of logistics is to ensure that the right products are delivered to the right place at the right time, in the right condition, and at the right cost. This requires a well-coordinated effort among different stakeholders, including suppliers, manufacturers, distributors, and retailers.

Transportation is one of the most visible and essential aspects of logistics. It involves the movement of goods from one location to another using various modes of transport, such as trucks, trains, ships, and airplanes. Efficient transportation is crucial for minimizing delivery times and costs. For example, in 2020, the global logistics market was valued at approximately $8.6 trillion, with transportation accounting for a significant portion of this value (Statista, 2021). Companies often use a combination of transportation modes to optimize their logistics operations, known as intermodal transportation. This approach can reduce costs and improve delivery times by leveraging the strengths of different transport modes. However, most logistics services involve either truck (illustrated in Figure 1 below) or ships.

Figure 1 Example of a truck (head)[1]

Logistics is the precise coordination of intricate processes involving personnel, infrastructure, and materials. It is frequently considered a component of supply chain management (SCM). Planning, carrying out, and managing the flow and storage of products, services, and information from the point of origin to the point of consumption are all included (Rushton et al., 2022). Better customer happiness, lower transportation costs, and better delivery performance can all result from effective logistics management. According to a study by the Logistics Management Association, "transportation costs account for approximately 60% of total logistics costs," highlighting the critical role of logistics in SCM.

---

[1] Source: https://www.rawpixel.com/, CC0 1.0

Warehousing is another vital component of logistics, involving the storage of goods until they are needed for production or sale. Effective warehousing strategies can help companies manage inventory levels, reduce storage costs, and improve order fulfillment rates. For instance, Amazon's extensive network of fulfillment centers allows the company to store products close to customers, enabling faster delivery times and enhancing customer satisfaction. In 2020, Amazon's logistics network included over 175 fulfillment centers worldwide, demonstrating the importance of warehousing in modern logistics (Amazon, 2020).

Inventory management is closely related to warehousing and involves the tracking and control of stock levels to ensure that products are available when needed without overstocking. For example, the just-in-time (JIT) inventory system, pioneered by Toyota, aims to reduce inventory levels by receiving goods only as they are needed in the production process. This approach has been widely adopted in various industries to improve efficiency and reduce costs (Li and Arreola-Risa, 2021, 2022).

Order fulfillment is the process of receiving, processing, and delivering customer orders. It involves several steps, including order picking, packing, and shipping. Efficient order fulfillment is crucial for meeting customer expectations and maintaining high levels of customer satisfaction. According to a survey by Deloitte, 73% of consumers consider fast and reliable delivery as a key factor in their purchasing decisions (Deloitte, 2020). Companies like Zappos have built their reputation on exceptional order fulfillment, offering free shipping and returns to enhance the customer experience.

In conclusion, logistics is a multifaceted discipline that plays a vital role in the success of supply chain management. By effectively managing transportation, warehousing, inventory, and order fulfillment, companies can improve efficiency, reduce costs, and enhance customer satisfaction. The integration of advanced technologies, such as automation and data analytics, is further transforming the logistics landscape, enabling companies to optimize their operations and stay competitive in an increasingly complex and dynamic market. An example of a logistics network is provided in Figure 2.

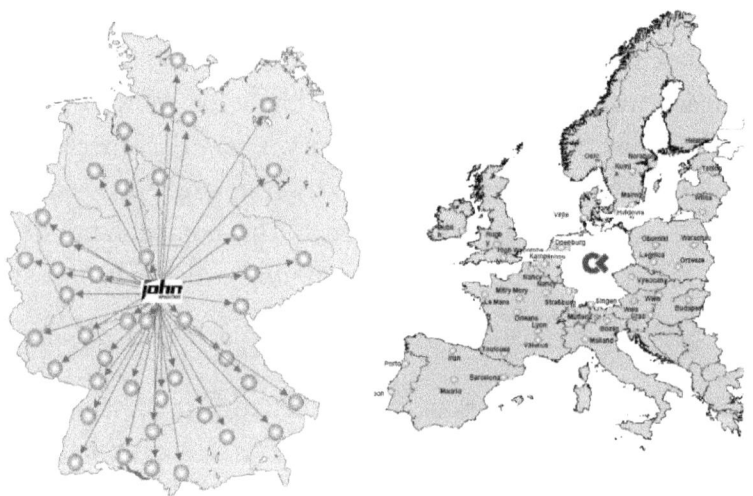

Figure 2 Example of a logistics network in Germany and Europe[2]

Definition and overview of edge computing

A disruptive computing paradigm known as edge computing has

---

[2] adapted from Wikipedia Commons, https://commons.wikimedia.org/wiki/File:CargoLine_LogisticsNetwork_John_Spedition_GmbH_Region_Fulda.jpg CC BY-SA 4.0

gained a lot of steam in recent years, mostly due to the quick spread of IoT devices and the growing need for real-time data. The explosion of data produced by networked devices has significantly contributed to the emergence of edge computing. With the proliferation of Internet of Things (IoT) devices, the volume of data generated has skyrocketed. According to the International Data Corporation (IDC), by 2025, there will be more than 150 billion connected devices worldwide, and 70% of IoT data will be processed at the network's edge (Patel et al., 2023). This massive influx of data has overwhelmed traditional cloud computing models, which struggle with bandwidth limitations, latency issues, and privacy concerns. Edge computing addresses these challenges by processing data closer to its source, thereby reducing latency and bandwidth usage while enhancing data security and privacy (Carvalho et al., 2021). The advent of 5G technology further amplifies the need for edge computing, as it enables faster data transmission and supports real-time applications such as autonomous vehicles, smart cities, and industrial automation. By 2025, it is estimated that edge computing will handle a significant portion of the data generated by these applications, ensuring efficient and timely processing (Patel et al., 2023). This shift towards edge computing not only optimizes network performance but also supports the growing demand for real-time data processing and analytics in various sectors.

Fundamentally, edge computing is the act of processing data closer to its source rather than relying solely on centralized cloud data centers. This localized technique reduces latency, bandwidth utilization, and allows for faster decision-making (Shi et al., 2016). Running calculations at the network's "edge" can help organizations enhance their ability to extract meaningful insights from data in real time and increase operational efficiency. These ''edges'' can be servers in mobile communication signal towers, local data centers, or users' devices. Conventional cloud computing systems usually struggle to handle such massive amounts of data since they rely on centralized data centers for processing. Latency difficulties, bandwidth limits, and the expenses of transferring massive datasets to cloud servers can all dramatically reduce performance and raise operational costs (Wang et al, 2023). Edge computing tackles these issues by enabling local data processing, which allows enterprises to study and act on data virtually instantly. Figure 3 illustrates how data flows in edge computing.

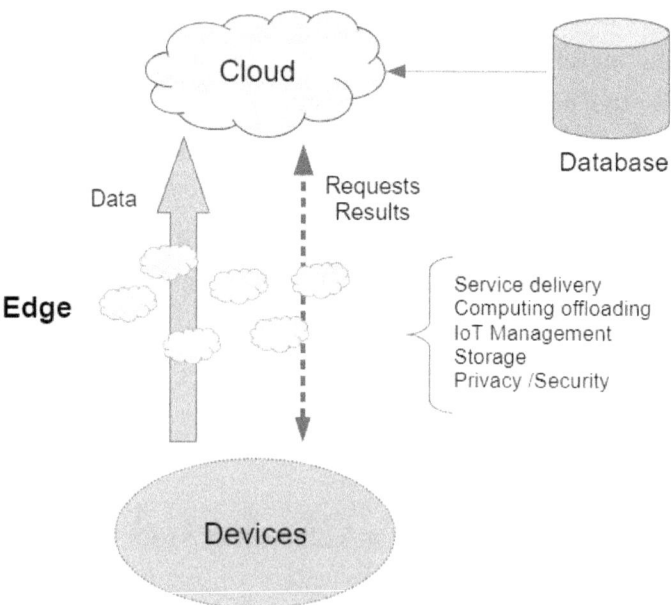

Figure 3 Example of edge computing data flow[3]

---

[3] source: Wikipedia,

One of the primary advantages of edge computing is its ability to facilitate real-time analytics, which is crucial for many modern applications. By processing data closer to its source, edge computing significantly reduces latency, enabling immediate data analysis and decision-making. This capability is particularly beneficial in scenarios where time-sensitive data is critical, such as in autonomous vehicles, industrial automation, and healthcare monitoring systems (Shi et al., 2016). For instance, in autonomous vehicles, real-time analytics can process sensor data on-the-fly to make split-second decisions, enhancing safety and efficiency. Similarly, in industrial settings, edge computing allows for real-time monitoring and predictive maintenance of machinery, reducing downtime and operational costs (Satyanarayanan, 2017). The healthcare sector also benefits from real-time analytics through edge computing, as it enables continuous monitoring of patients' vital signs and immediate response to any anomalies, thereby improving patient outcomes. According to a report by Gartner, by 2025, 75% of enterprise-generated data will be created and processed outside a traditional centralized data center or cloud, underscoring the growing importance of edge computing in real-time analytics (Gartner, 2021). This shift not only enhances the speed and efficiency of data processing but also supports the increasing demand for real-time insights in various industries.

Edge computing is often discussed in conjunction with related concepts such as fog computing and mist computing, each playing a crucial role in the broader landscape of distributed computing.

---

https://upload.wikimedia.org/wikipedia/commons/3/34/Edge_computing_paradigm%2C_2019-07-03.svg, CC BY-NC 2.0

Edge computing involves processing data at or near the source of data generation, reducing latency and bandwidth usage. Fog computing extends this concept by creating a network of nodes that process data between the edge devices and the cloud, providing an additional layer of data processing and storage (Chiang & Zhang, 2016). This intermediate layer helps in managing the data flow more efficiently, especially in scenarios requiring real-time analytics and decision-making. Mist computing, on the other hand, takes the concept even further by pushing computational tasks to the very edge of the network, often directly onto the IoT devices themselves (Varghese & Buyya, 2018). This approach minimizes latency to the lowest possible levels and is particularly useful for applications requiring immediate data processing, such as in healthcare monitoring systems or autonomous vehicles. The synergy between these computing paradigms allows for a more flexible and scalable infrastructure, capable of handling the massive amounts of data generated by modern IoT ecosystems. By leveraging the strengths of edge, fog, and mist computing, organizations can optimize their data processing strategies, ensuring that critical data is processed quickly and efficiently while less urgent data can be handled by the cloud.

One significant challenge is the shortage of skilled professionals who can manage and maintain edge computing infrastructure. As the technology landscape evolves rapidly, companies must ensure they possess the expertise to develop, operate, and troubleshoot edge computing solutions. This often requires substantial investment in staff training or hiring experts, which can be particularly costly for smaller firms or those with limited resources (Akbari, 2023). For example, a small manufacturing company might struggle to implement edge computing for real-time monitoring of their production line due to the high costs associated with training existing staff or hiring new specialists. This financial burden can hinder their ability to leverage the full benefits of edge computing technology.

Furthermore, because edge computing devices frequently work in diverse and occasionally severe environments, assuring their dependability and security becomes critical. Edge devices are susceptible to physical dangers, climatic conditions, and cyber-attacks, necessitating strong security measures and maintenance plans (Wang et al, 2023). Organizations must establish end-to-end security measures that safeguard data in transit and at rest, especially since edge devices might serve as possible entry points for cyber threats. This is especially important in logistics management, where data integrity and confidentiality are key to building confidence with partners and stakeholders. The dependability and security concerns can be addressed through standardization, which remains a significant issue in edge computing. The lack of universally accepted standards for edge device communication and data formats can complicate integration efforts, making it challenging for organizations to adopt edge computing solutions that work seamlessly across their existing systems (Bonomi et al., 2012). Efforts to establish common standards and protocols will be essential for facilitating broader adoption and interoperability of edge computing technologies.

To sum up, edge computing signifies a paradigm change in the way businesses handle data processing and analysis, especially when it comes to logistics. Edge computing lowers latency, improves operational efficiency, and allows real-time analytics by moving computation closer to the data source. In addition to facilitating prompt decision-making, local data processing lowers bandwidth expenses and enhances data security. However, thorough consideration of the difficulties involved—such as technology integration, staff training, reliability, and standardization—is necessary for the successful implementation of edge computing solutions. Logistics management will probably see a rise in the use of edge computing as sectors continue to change and adjust to the demands of the digital era. Businesses that successfully use edge computing will be in a better position to increase customer happiness, boost operational efficiency, and hold onto a competitive edge in a market that is changing quickly. Therefore, for businesses hoping to prosper in the age of digital transformation, investigating edge computing technologies in logistics management is not only appropriate but also crucial.

Edge computing in logistics

By facilitating real-time logistics process monitoring, analysis, and control, edge computing presents several benefits for logistics management. A product or service is supplied to a customer through a complex web of organizations, individuals, activities, information, and resources known as the logistics. The demand for quicker delivery times and globalization have made logistics more complex, necessitating the development of novel technical solutions. By enabling the quick analysis of data produced at different stages of the logistics, edge computing offers a potent instrument to address these issues (Akbari, 2023).

For instance, in manufacturing, edge computing can enable predictive maintenance of machinery by continuously analyzing data from sensors embedded in equipment. This approach allows organizations to anticipate equipment failures and perform maintenance proactively, thus avoiding costly downtimes and optimizing operational efficiency (Wang et al, 2023). Furthermore, edge devices can monitor production lines in real time, detecting anomalies and ensuring that quality standards are consistently met. This capability not only enhances productivity but also contributes to increased customer satisfaction, as products are delivered with greater reliability and quality.

Edge computing is essential for maintaining inventory levels and tracking shipments in logistics and transportation. Businesses can get real-time visibility into the location and state of items in transit by employing edge devices that are GPS and RFID enabled. This data is crucial for logistics disruption response, delivery time improvement, and routing optimization (Akbari, 2023). Furthermore, edge computing can help with improved inventory management by giving precise information on turnover rates and stock levels, which empowers businesses to decide how best to allocate their inventory and refill. Moreover, edge computing enhances data security and privacy—critical considerations in logistics management, where sensitive information is often exchanged. By processing data locally, organizations can mitigate the risk of exposing sensitive information to potential breaches during data transmission to centralized cloud servers. This localized approach allows for the implementation of robust security measures at the edge, ultimately safeguarding critical business data (Wang et al, 2023). Organizations can leverage edge computing to enforce stringent access controls and data encryption techniques, thereby ensuring compliance challenges. Organizations must navigate a complex landscape of hardware and software requirements to implement computing solutions effectively. The integration of diverse, legacy systems, and varying communication protocols can pose significant obstacles in achieving seamless data flow and interoperability within the logistics (Cao et al., 2020). Additionally, the decentralized nature of edge computing necessitates a robust infrastructure to ensure that edge nodes can communicate effectively with one another and with centralized cloud services when necessary.

References:

Akbari, M. (2023). Revolutionizing supply chain and circular economy with edge computing: Systematic review, research themes and future directions. *Management Decision*. In press. https://doi.org/10.1108/MD-03-2023-0412

Amazon. (2020). Amazon fulfillment center network. Retrieved from https://www.aboutamazon.com/news/operations/amazon-fulfillment-center-network

Bonomi, F., Milito, R., Zhu, J., & Addepalli, S. (2012). Fog computing and its role in the internet of things. In *Proceedings of the first edition of the MCC workshop on Mobile cloud computing* (pp. 13-16).

Cao, K., Liu, Y., Meng, G., & Sun, Q. (2020). An overview on edge computing research. *IEEE access, 8*, 85714-85728.

Carvalho, G., Cabral, B., Pereira, V., & Bernardino, J. (2021). Edge computing: Current trends, research challenges and future directions. *Computing, 103*(7), 993-1023. https://doi.org/10.1007/s00607-020-00896-5

Chiang, M., & Zhang, T. (2016). Fog and IoT: An overview of research opportunities. *IEEE Internet of Things Journal, 3*(6), 854-864. https://doi.org/10.1109/JIOT.2016.2584538

Deloitte. (2020). The consumer is changing, but perhaps not how you think. Retrieved from https://www2.deloitte.com/us/en/insights/industry/retail-distribution/future-of-consumer.html

Gartner. (2021). Gartner says the future of cloud is at the edge. Retrieved from https://www.gartner.com/en/newsroom/press-releases/2021-10-18-gartner-says-the-future-of-cloud-is-at-the-edge

Li, B., & Arreola-Risa, A. (2021). On minimizing downside risk in make-to-stock, risk-averse firms. *Naval Research Logistics (NRL), 68*(2), 199-213.

Li, B., & Arreola-Risa, A. (2022). Minimizing conditional value-at-risk under a modified basestock policy. *Production and Operations Management, 31*(4), 1822-1838.

Patel, R., Prasad, L., Tandon, R., & Rathore, N. P. S. (2023). A comprehensive review on edge computing, applications & challenges. In *Security and Risk Analysis for Intelligent Edge Computing* (pp. 1-33). Springer. https://doi.org/10.1007/978-3-031-28150-1_1

Rushton, A., Croucher, P., & Baker, P. (2022). *The handbook of logistics and distribution management: Understanding the supply chain*. Kogan Page Publishers.

Satyanarayanan, M. (2017). The emergence of edge computing. *Computer, 50*(1), 30-39. https://doi.org/10.1109/MC.2017.9

Shi, W., Cao, J., Zhang, Q., Li, Y., & Xu, L. D. (2016). Edge computing: Vision and challenges. *IEEE Internet of Things Journal, 3*(5), 637-646.

Statista. (2021). Global logistics market size 2020. Retrieved from https://www.statista.com/statistics/1106364/global-logistics-market-size/

Varghese, B., & Buyya, R. (2018). Next generation cloud computing: New trends and research directions. *Future Generation Computer Systems, 79*, 849-861. https://doi.org/10.1016/j.future.2017.09.020

Wang, T., Liang, Y., Shen, X., Zheng, X., Mahmood, A., & Sheng, Q. Z. (2023). Edge computing and sensor-cloud: Overview, solutions, and directions. ACM Computing Surveys, 55(13s), 1-37.

THE EDGE COMPUTING TECHNOLOGY

In this chapter, we provide an overview of the edge computing technology.

Fundamental principles of edge computing

Edge computing is a transformative to data processing that emphasizes decentralization, enabling data to be processed closer to its source rather than relying solely on centralized cloud infrastructures. The fundamental principles of edge computing revolve around reducing latency, optimizing bandwidth usage, enhancing data security, and facilitating real-time analytics. By placing computational resources at the "edge" of the network—near the data source—organizations can achieve faster response times and improved performance for applications that require immediate data processing. This design is particularly beneficial for scenarios involving Internet of Things (IoT) devices, autonomous systems, and real-time analytics, where even minimal delays can lead to significant inefficiencies or safety risks (Shi et al., 2016).

The origins of edge computing may be traced back to the early 2000s, when the proliferation of IoT devices began to change the data collection and processing landscape. The initial concept of edge computing arose in response to the constraints presented by traditional cloud computing infrastructures, which were largely built for static data processing. As the number of connected devices grew, it became evident that a more agile and efficient method was required to manage the massive amounts of data generated (Wang et al, 2023). In this setting, edge computing gained popularity as a feasible solution to the limits of centralized computing. The phrase "edge computing" first gained popularity in the early 2010s, particularly in the telecommunications industry, which identified the benefits of deploying computing resources closer to the network edge to improve service delivery and minimize latency. Telecommunications firms began to investigate the concept to improve the performance of mobile networks, especially with the introduction of 4G and eventually 5G technologies. The deployment of these networks resulted in a large rise in linked devices and data traffic, emphasizing the importance of localized processing capabilities (Cao et al., 2020). These advancements lead to the possibility of running web application on the edge (see Figure 4).

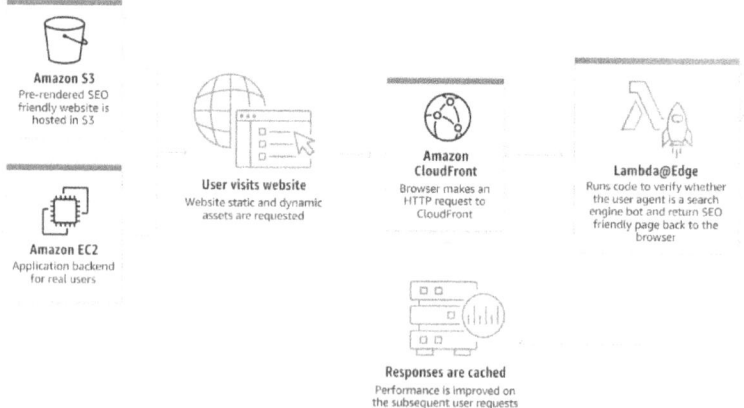

Figure 4 Example of search engine optimization using edge computing[4]

---

[4] source: https://aws.amazon.com/lambda/edge/?nc1=h_ls, CC BY-NC 2.0

Edge computing started to find uses in a variety of industries, such as manufacturing, healthcare, transportation, and smart cities, as the IoT landscape continued to change. In addition to lowering latency, local data processing also eased bandwidth restrictions and enhanced data security and privacy. For example, edge computing can be used more successfully in the healthcare industry to enable real-time monitoring of patient vital signs using wearable devices, allowing for quick notifications for severe conditions without the latency associated with transferring data to centralized servers (Akbari, 2023).

By 2017, edge computing had firmly established itself as a pivotal element of modern IT infrastructure. According to a report by Gartner, it was projected that by 2025, over 75% of enterprise-generated data would be processed outside traditional centralized data centers. This statistic highlights the growing recognition of edge computing as a fundamental enabler of digital transformation, particularly as organizations increasingly adopt IoT technologies. Edge computing helps to increase data governance and compliance in addition to processing data closer to the source. Organizations can reduce the risk of data breaches and guarantee compliance with regulations by storing critical data locally. This is especially important in industries like banking and healthcare where protecting and privatizing data is crucial (Wang et al, 2023). Moreover, edge computing facilitates increased flexibility and resilience in digital ecosystems by supporting the trend toward decentralized applications and services.

The adoption of edge computing has been expedited by its convergence with other developing technologies, like machine learning (ML) and artificial intelligence (AI). Organizations can use real-time data analytics and AI algorithms to automate processes and make well-informed decisions by combining edge devices with data. Predictive maintenance, for instance, can be used in the manufacturing industry to help companies anticipate equipment breakdowns and minimize downtime by continuously evaluating data from sensors integrated into machinery (Cao et al., 2020).

Despite its numerous advantages, implementing edge computing is challenging. Organizations must navigate a complex landscape of hardware and software requirements, as well as varying communication protocols and standards. The integration of edge computing solutions with existing IT infrastructure can pose significant obstacles, particularly for organizations with legacy systems (Bonomi et al., 2012). Additionally, the need for skilled personnel to manage and maintain edge computing infrastructure can be a barrier to widespread adoption.

Implementing edge computing presents several significant challenges, as highlighted by Cao, Liu, Meng, and Sun (2020). One of the primary issues is the heterogeneity of edge devices. These devices vary widely in terms of processing power, storage capacity, and communication capabilities, making it difficult to develop standardized solutions that can be universally applied. Moreover, the deployment of edge computing raises concerns related to standardization and interoperability. As multiple vendors offer edge computing solutions, the lack of universally accepted standards can lead to compatibility issues, making it difficult for organizations to integrate different technologies seamlessly. This fragmentation can hinder the scalability of edge computing solutions and complicate maintenance and support, thereby limiting their effectiveness in logistics applications (Bonomi et al., 2012). The management of data privacy and regulatory compliance presents another major challenge. Organizations must be aware of the legal ramifications of data collecting, processing, and storage as they depend more and more on real-time data analytics for decision-making. Edge computing solutions must have strong data governance frameworks to ensure compliance with regulations like the General Data Protection Regulation (GDPR) in Europe, which place strict guidelines on how businesses handle personal data (Wang et al, 2023). As a result, companies need to give top priority to data management procedures that meet both legal and operational criteria.

Moreover, network connectivity remains a significant challenge, particularly in remote or underserved regions where stable and high-speed internet connections are often lacking. This can result in inconsistent performance and reliability issues. Security and privacy are also critical concerns, as edge devices frequently handle sensitive data. Implementing robust security measures to protect against cyber threats while maintaining user privacy is both complex and resource intensive. Additionally, resource management at the edge is a crucial challenge. Efficiently allocating and managing limited computational resources to handle dynamic workloads requires sophisticated algorithms and strategies. The interoperability between various edge computing platforms and existing cloud infrastructure presents another obstacle, necessitating seamless integration to ensure smooth data flow and processing. Finally, scalability is a major issue, as the deployment of edge computing solutions must be scalable to accommodate the growing number of IoT devices and the increasing volume of data they generate. Addressing these challenges requires ongoing research and development to create more resilient, secure, and efficient edge computing systems (Cao et al., 2020).

Despite these challenges, the potential of edge computing to transform logistics is substantial. The advantages of lower latency, reduced bandwidth consumption, enhanced data security, and real-time analytics make edge computing an attractive option for organizations aiming to optimize their logistics operations. As technology advances, we can anticipate increased investments in edge computing infrastructure, leading to improvements in capabilities and more widespread adoption across various industries (Akbari, 2023).

In summary, edge computing represents a fundamental shift in how businesses process and evaluate data within the logistics context. Localized data processing enables enterprises to leverage real-time analytics to enhance operational efficiency, decision-making, and market response time. However, the successful adoption of edge computing solutions requires addressing several issues, including integration complexity, data privacy concerns, and the need for standardization. As enterprises navigate this evolving landscape, edge computing is poised to play a crucial role in modernizing logistics, making it more agile, efficient, and responsive to the demands of the modern marketplace.

Edge devices and architecture

The architecture of edge computing is composed of various components, including edge devices, edge gateways, and the network infrastructure that connects them. Understanding components is essential for the full potential of computing in various applications, particularly in logistics. An example is provided in Figure 5.

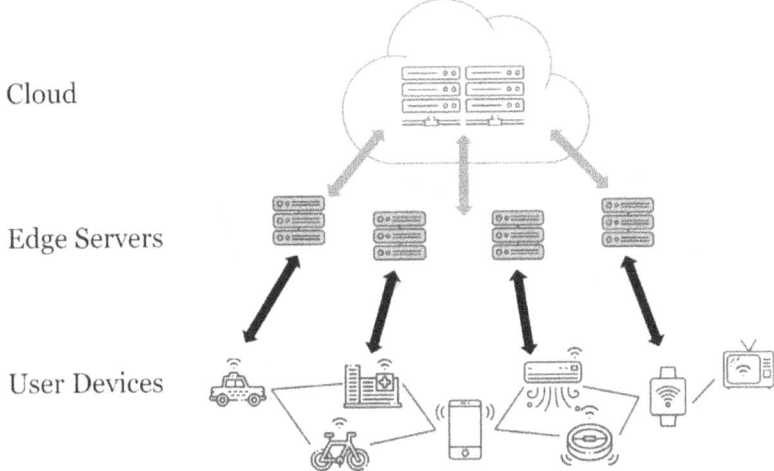

Figure 5 Basic representation of edge-cloud architecture[5]

Edge devices

Edge devices form the backbone of edge computing architecture, tasked with the collection, processing, and analysis of data at or near its source. Examples of these devices include sensors, IoT gadgets, cameras, and local servers (see Figure 6). Gartner's report projects that by 2025, more than 75% of enterprise-generated data will be created and processed outside centralized data centers (Gartner, 2021). This underscores the growing dependence on edge devices for data generation and processing.

---

[5] Adapted from Wikipedia, https://encrypted-tbn0.gstatic.com/images?q=tbn:ANd9GcQW5eboIYthJp5GH2LyHs6-Uhm9JEK0j7wF-w&s, CC BY-NC 2.0

Figure 6 An edge server

In various industries, sensors and IoT devices play pivotal roles. For instance, in manufacturing, sensors attached to machinery can monitor performance metrics such as temperature, vibration, and operational speed in real-time. This data can be locally processed to detect anomalies and trigger alerts before issues escalate, facilitating predictive maintenance and minimizing downtime (Wang et al., 2023). Similarly, in logistics, GPS and RFID-enabled devices can track the location and condition of shipments, providing valuable insights for inventory management and enhancing logistics efficiency.

Edge gateways

Edge gateways act as intermediaries between edge devices and the cloud or central data centers. They aggregate data from multiple edge devices, perform initial processing, and filter out unnecessary information before transmitting relevant data to the cloud for further analysis. This architecture reduces the volume of data sent to centralized systems, alleviating bandwidth strain and minimizing latency (Bonomi et al., 2012). Additionally, edge gateways can enhance security by serving as a barrier between edge devices and external networks. They can implement security protocols, such as firewalls and encryption, to protect sensitive data transmitted from edge devices (Cao et al., 2020). This added layer of security is particularly crucial in logistics management, where confidential information about products and logistics is frequently exchanged.

Network infrastructure and models

A crucial aspect of edge computing design is the network infrastructure, which ensures seamless communication between edge devices, gateways, and cloud services. This architecture typically employs a mix of wired and wireless communication technologies, such as Wi-Fi, cellular networks (including 4G and 5G), and low-power wide-area networks (LPWAN). The choice of communication technology depends on the application's specific requirements, such as data transfer speed, range, and power consumption (Akbari, 2023). The advent of 5G technology has significantly influenced edge computing by providing faster data transfer rates, reduced latency, and increased capacity to connect more devices. 5G facilitates real-time communication between edge devices and central systems, enabling quicker decision-making and more efficient data processing (Wang et al., 2023). For example, 5G-enabled edge computing can support applications like public safety and traffic control in smart cities by analyzing data from multiple sensors and cameras in real time. Las Vegas has implemented this technology with edge-computing-enabled traffic lights to monitor traffic conditions (Raynovich, 2020).

Edge computing architecture can be categorized into several models based on the distribution of computing resources and the degree of centralization. The two most common models are centralized and decentralized architectures.

1. Centralized Architecture: In a centralized edge computing architecture, data is processed at a single edge location or gateway before being sent to the cloud. This model is often suitable for applications with less stringent latency requirements, as it allows for easier management and maintenance of edge devices. However, it may introduce bottlenecks in data processing if the centralized edge device becomes overloaded with data.

2. Decentralized Architecture: Conversely, a decentralized architecture distributes processing power among multiple gateways and edge devices. This architecture enhances fault tolerance, as the failure of a single device does not compromise the entire system. Additionally, it enables parallel processing of data streams from various sources, leading to more efficient data processing (Cao et al., 2020). Applications requiring real-time analytics, such as industrial automation and autonomous vehicles, benefit significantly from this design, as it allows data to be processed instantly, ensuring efficiency and safety.

Integration with cloud computing

Although edge computing concentrates on processing data locally, it is not a stand-alone system. Rather, it's intended to work in tandem with cloud computing, forming a hybrid architecture that makes use of both paradigms' advantages. Under this hybrid paradigm, the cloud acts as a centralized repository for complex analytics and long-term data storage, while edge devices perform time-sensitive data processing (Akbari, 2023). An illustration of cloud computing use cases is provided in Figure 7.

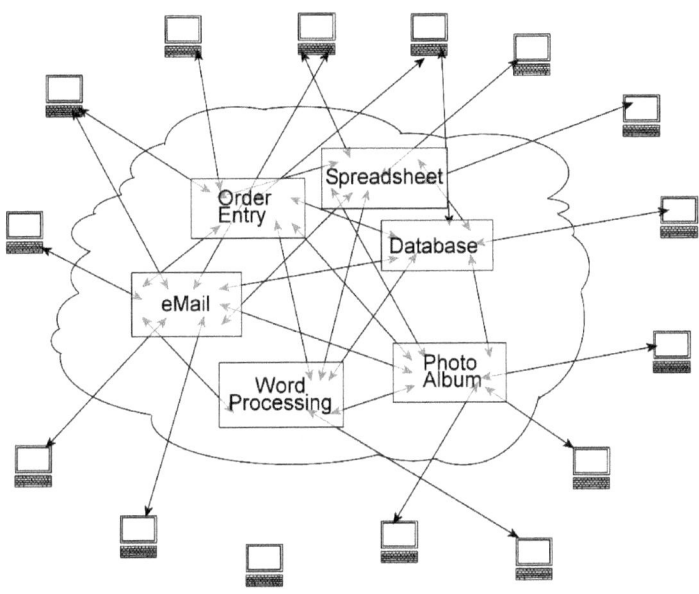

Figure 7 An illustration of cloud computing use cases[6]

For instance, in logistics management, edge devices can monitor inventory levels in real time, while the cloud can analyze historical data to forecast demand challenges. Organizations must navigate a complex landscape of hardware and software requirements to implement computing solutions effectively. The integration of diverse devices legacy systems, and varying communication protocols can pose significant obstacles. Additionally, organizations need to ensure they possess the necessary skills and expertise to manage and maintain edge computing infrastructure,

---

[6] Source: https://upload.wikimedia.org/wikipedia/en/b/be/Cloud_Computing.jpg, , CC BY-NC 2.0

which may require training existing staff or hiring new talent (Cao et al., 2020).

Moreover, the deployment of edge computing solutions necessitates careful planning and investment. Organizations must assess their specific needs, determine the optimal placement of edge devices, and evaluate the potential return on investment. As with any technology implementation, there is a risk of obsolescence or incompatibility with future systems, which can complicate the decision-making process (Bonomi et al., 2012). Furthermore, organizations must also consider the regulatory requirements surrounding data privacy and security, particularly when dealing with sensitive information in logistics operations.

The advantages of edge computing for logistics management are significant, notwithstanding these difficulties. Edge computing can result in increased customer happiness, lower costs, and better operational efficiency by providing real-time data processing and analytics. The incorporation of edge computing into logistics operations is expected to become a crucial differentiation in a competitive market as businesses embrace digital transformation more and more.

To sum up, edge computing is a big step forward in terms of how businesses handle and use data. Edge computing overcomes the drawbacks of traditional cloud computing by decentralizing data processing and moving computation closer to the point of data generation. This allows for real-time analytics and decision-making. Edge computing has significant implications for logistics management, enabling firms to boost visibility, improve operational efficiency, and react quickly to shifting market demands. Understanding and utilizing edge computing will be crucial for businesses looking to keep a competitive edge in their markets as the technological landscape changes further.

Edge computing and cloud computing

Edge computing and cloud computing are two complementary paradigms that play pivotal roles in modern data management and processing. While they share some similarities, they differ significantly in architecture, functionality, and their respective use cases. Understanding these differences and connections is essential for organizations looking to optimize their IT strategies and leverage the advantages of both models. Edge computing can be categorized into five types:

- ✧ Service provide edge
  - ■ Regional edge: regional servers
  - ■ Access Edge: in telecommunication networks.
- ✧ User edge
  - ■ On-premises data center edge: often used in manufacturing plants, retail, and logistics locations
  - ■ Smart device edge: processing at smart devices (routers, smart speakers, etc.)
  - ■ Constrained device edge: micro-controllers such as light switches.

Differences in architecture and data processing

The architectural frameworks of edge computing and cloud computing differ significantly. Cloud computing relies on centralized data centers to process and store large volumes of data. Due to the physical distance between the data source and the cloud server, users may experience higher latency when transferring data to these remote data centers for processing (Cao et al., 2020). In contrast, edge computing decentralizes data processing by bringing it closer to the "edge" of the network, where the data is generated. This design significantly reduces latency and improves response times by enabling real-time data processing (Shi et al., 2016).

For instance, in a smart manufacturing environment, a cloud-based system would require all data generated by machinery to be sent to a centralized server for analysis. This could lead to delays in identifying equipment failures or production anomalies. Conversely, edge computing allows local devices to analyze data in real time, enabling immediate corrective actions and reducing costly downtime. According to a report by Gartner (2020), organizations that implement edge computing can achieve latency reductions of up to 75%, thereby enhancing operational efficiency.

The differences in architecture and data processing capabilities also lead to distinct use cases for edge and cloud computing. Cloud computing is well-suited for applications that require extensive data storage, complex analytics, and high computational power, such as big data analytics, machine learning model training, and data archiving. Organizations often leverage cloud computing for tasks that do not require immediate responses or real-time processing (Bonomi et al., 2012). Conversely, edge computing is particularly advantageous in scenarios that demand real-time analytics and low latency. Use cases such as autonomous vehicles, smart cities, and industrial automation benefit significantly from edge computing's ability to process data at the source. For example, an autonomous vehicle must process data from its sensors in milliseconds to make split-second decisions. In this context, edge computing is essential for ensuring safety and operational efficiency (Cao et al., 2020).

Data management and bandwidth efficiency

The approaches to data management and bandwidth consumption in cloud and edge computing differ significantly. Cloud computing often requires substantial bandwidth to transfer large volumes of data to and from centralized servers. According to Wang et al. (2023), this can lead to network congestion and increased data transfer costs. In contrast, edge computing processes and filters data locally, reducing the amount of data that needs to be transmitted over the network. This approach optimizes bandwidth usage and lowers associated costs by sending only relevant insights or aggregated data to the cloud for further analysis or storage (Akbari, 2023). For example, in Internet of Things (IoT) applications, edge devices can preprocess sensor data to extract essential information, such as anomalies or trends. This not only decreases the volume of data sent to the cloud but also improves the overall system's responsiveness and performance. Cisco (2021) reports that by 2025, approximately 75% of enterprise-generated data will be created and processed outside centralized data centers, underscoring the growing importance of edge computing in efficient data management.

The architectural and data processing differences between cloud and edge computing lead to distinct use cases. Cloud computing is ideal for applications requiring extensive data storage, complex analytics, and high computational power, such as big data analytics, machine learning model training, and data archiving. Organizations often use cloud computing for tasks that do not need immediate responses or real-time processing (Bonomi et al., 2012).

Conversely, edge computing excels in scenarios demanding real-time analytics and low latency. Applications like autonomous vehicles, smart cities, and industrial automation benefit greatly from edge computing's ability to process data at the source. For instance, an autonomous vehicle must process sensor data within milliseconds to make split-second decisions, making edge computing crucial for ensuring safety and operational efficiency (Cao et al., 2020).

Connections and complementarity

Despite their differences, edge computing and cloud computing are complementary technologies that work together to enhance data processing capabilities rather than being opposing forces. Organizations often adopt a hybrid architecture to optimize their operations by leveraging both cloud and edge computing. In this model, cloud computing provides additional layers of storage, analytics, and machine learning capabilities for aggregated data, while edge computing handles real-time data processing and analysis (Wang et al., 2023). For example, a retail organization might use edge computing to process data from point-of-sale systems in real time to manage inventory levels and customer transactions. Simultaneously, the organization could utilize cloud computing to analyze aggregated sales data over time to identify trends and inform strategic business decisions. This hybrid approach allows organizations to capitalize on the strengths of both paradigms.

While edge computing and cloud computing differ in their architectural frameworks, data processing approaches, and use cases, they are interconnected in a way that allows organizations to optimize their data management strategies effectively. As the volume of data generated by IoT devices continues to grow, the importance of edge computing in complementing cloud services will only increase. By understanding the differences and connections between these two paradigms, organizations can make informed decisions about how best to leverage their capabilities.

Organizations must navigate a complex landscape of hardware and software requirements to implement edge computing solutions effectively. The integration of diverse devices, legacy systems, and varying communication protocols can pose significant obstacles. Additionally, organizations need to ensure that they have the necessary skills and expertise to manage and maintain edge computing infrastructure (Cao et al., 2020). Successful implementation requires careful planning, investment, and a clear understanding of the specific needs of the supply chain. Another challenge lies in the fragmentation of edge computing solutions, where multiple vendors and technologies exist. The lack of standardization in edge computing architectures can lead to interoperability issues, making it difficult for organizations to integrate their existing systems with new edge computing technologies (Akbari, 2023). Consequently, businesses may find themselves locked into specific vendor ecosystems.

Moreover, while edge computing offers enhanced data security benefits, it also raises new cybersecurity concerns. With data being processed on numerous edge devices spread across various locations, the attack surface for potential cyber threats increases significantly (Wang et al., 2023). Organizations must implement robust security protocols to protect edge devices and the data they handle, including encryption, access controls, and continuous monitoring. This necessitates a shift in cybersecurity strategies, as traditional perimeter-based security measures may not be adequate for a decentralized edge computing environment (Cao et al., 2020). A summary table is provided below in Table 1.

Table 1 Differences Between Edge Computing and Cloud Computing

Aspect	Edge Computing	Cloud Computing
Architecture	Decentralized, processing at the data source	Centralized, processing in remote data centers
Latency	Low latency due to proximity to data source	Higher latency due to distance from data source
Data Processing	Real-time processing and analysis	Batch processing and complex analytics
Use Cases	Real-time applications (e.g., autonomous vehicles)	Extensive data storage and analytics (e.g., big data)
Bandwidth Usage	Reduced by local processing	High due to large data transfers
Scalability	Limited by local resources	Highly scalable with cloud resources
Security	Enhanced security but increased attack surface	Centralized security measures
Operational Efficiency	Immediate corrective actions and reduced downtime	Long-term data analysis and strategic decisions

Despite these challenges, edge computing has the potential to revolutionize logistics. Businesses that successfully implement edge computing can enhance customer satisfaction, improve operational efficiency, and drive innovation to gain a competitive edge.

References:

Akbari, M. (2023). Revolutionizing supply chain and circular economy with edge computing: Systematic review, research themes and future directions. *Management Decision*. In press. https://doi.org/10.1108/MD-03-2023-0412

Bonomi, F., Milito, R., Zhu, J., & Addepalli, S. (2012). Fog computing and its role in the internet of things. In *Proceedings of the first edition of the MCC workshop on Mobile cloud computing* (pp. 13-16).

Cao, K., Liu, Y., Meng, G., & Sun, Q. (2020). An overview on edge computing research. *IEEE Access*, *8*, 85714-85728.

Cisco. (2021). A guide to successful edge computing deployments. Cisco. Retrieved from https://www.cisco.com/c/dam/en/us/solutions/global-partners/edge-computing-deployments-guide.pdf

Gartner. (2020). Hype Cycle for Edge Computing, 2020. Gartner. Retrieved from https://www.gartner.com/en/documents/3989981

Raynovich, R. S. (2020). Edge case study: Inside the Las Vegas smart city. Futuriom. Retrieved from https://www.futuriom.com/articles/news/edge-case-study-inside-the-las-vegas-smart-city/2020/02

Shi, W., Cao, J., Zhang, Q., Li, Y., & Xu, L. (2016). Edge computing: Vision and challenges. *IEEE Internet of Things Journal, 3*(5), 637-646.

Shi, W., & Dustdar, S. (2016). The promise of edge computing. *Computer, 49*(5), 78-81.

Statista. (2021). Number of connected devices worldwide from 2012 to 2030. Retrieved from https://www.statista.com/statistics/802383/worldwide-connected-devices/

Wang, T., Liang, Y., Shen, X., Zheng, X., Mahmood, A., & Sheng, Q. Z. (2023). Edge computing and sensor-cloud: Overview, solutions, and directions. ACM Computing Surveys, 55(13s), 1-37.

DATA PROCESSING IN LOGISTICS

In this chapter, we review the data flow in logistics and how to manage them.

Data collection

In the modern landscape of logistics, effective data collection is fundamental to operational efficiency and strategic decision-making. The integration of sensors and Application Programming Interfaces (APIs) has revolutionized how businesses gather and utilize data, enabling real-time insights and enhanced visibility across logistics networks. This section explores the significance of data collection through sensors and APIs, the technologies involved, and the challenges and opportunities presented by these innovations.

One significant tool that has emerged to facilitate data collection in logistics is the Internet of Things (IoT). IoT devices, equipped with sensors, monitor various parameters along the supply chain, such as temperature, humidity, and location. For instance, temperature sensors are widely used in the food and pharmaceutical logistics to ensure goods are transported and stored in controlled environments. According to a report by Markets and Markets (2020), the global IoT in supply chain market is projected to grow at a compound annual growth rate (CAGR) of 17.4%, from $40.4 billion in 2020 to $88.1 billion by 2025. This growth underscores the increasing reliance on IoT technologies for efficient data collection. GPS sensors enable real-time tracking of shipments, allowing businesses to monitor the location of goods in transit. This capability is crucial for optimizing transportation routes and reducing delays. A study by the American Transportation Research Institute (2021) found that improving the efficiency of freight movement could save the U.S. economy up to $42 billion annually. By leveraging sensor data, companies can make informed decisions that enhance overall logistics performance.

APIs further enhance the data collection process by enabling the seamless transfer of data between various systems. APIs facilitate communication between disparate software applications, allowing companies to compile information from a range of sources, such as suppliers, shipping companies, and inventory management systems. For example, retailers can use APIs to retrieve real-time inventory data from suppliers, facilitating prompt restocking and minimizing stockouts. According to a survey by MuleSoft (2020), 89% of businesses have implemented APIs to increase data integration and operational efficiency. In addition to streamlining data collection, the ability to connect systems via APIs improves the accuracy and reliability of the information obtained.

While there are numerous advantages to using sensors and APIs for data collection, companies also face several challenges. One major obstacle is the enormous amount of data generated by IoT devices. As logistics become more complex, businesses may struggle to organize and analyze the vast volumes of information collected. According to an IDC study (IDC, 2020), the global datasphere is expected to reach 175 zettabytes by 2025, highlighting the need for advanced data management solutions. To address this issue, organizations must invest in data management platforms capable of efficiently collecting, handling, and analyzing data from multiple sources.

Additionally, the diversity of data formats and sources can complicate data integration efforts. Sensors from different manufacturers may produce data in varying formats, making it challenging to consolidate the information for analysis. To overcome this challenge, organizations should adopt standardized data formats and protocols to facilitate smoother data integration and interoperability. Implementing data normalization techniques can also help ensure that data from disparate sources can be analyzed cohesively (Li, 2009).

Furthermore, the privacy and security of data collected by sensors and APIs are critical concerns. As reliance on connected devices increases, so does the risk of cyberattacks and data breaches. The Cybersecurity & Infrastructure Security Agency (CISA) has identified logistics as a primary target for cyberattacks, emphasizing the need for robust security measures (CISA, 2022). Organizations must implement encryption methods, access controls, and monitoring systems to protect sensitive information gathered by IoT devices and APIs.

Another crucial aspect of data collection is compliance with data privacy regulations. As organizations gather vast amounts of data, they must ensure their practices align with legal requirements such as the General Data Protection Regulation (GDPR) in the European Union. Compliance not only protects organizations from legal repercussions but also fosters trust among customers and partners. A study by PwC (2021) found that 85% of consumers desire greater control over their personal data, highlighting the importance of transparency and ethical data practices.

In summary, data collection via sensors and APIs significantly enhances logistics. The integration of IoT devices enables real-time monitoring of critical metrics, promoting efficient operations and informed decision-making. APIs streamline data transfer between various systems, allowing businesses to fully leverage their data. To maximize the benefits of these technologies, companies must address challenges related to data volume, format diversity, security, and compliance. By investing in data management solutions and implementing best practices for data collection and integration, organizations can increase the visibility and responsiveness of their logistics, leading to higher customer satisfaction and a competitive edge.

Furthermore, as organizations increasingly adopt advanced analytics and machine learning techniques, the data collected from sensors and APIs can be used to derive predictive insights that drive strategic decisions. For example, analytics can identify patterns in historical data to forecast demand fluctuations, enabling businesses to optimize inventory levels and reduce excess stock. According to a report by McKinsey (2022), companies that use advanced analytics in their logistics can achieve a 10-20% reduction in logistics costs. By leveraging the rich data collected through sensors and APIs, organizations can transition from reactive to proactive logistics.

The importance of real-time data collection cannot be overstated. In a dynamic marketplace, having access to current data enables organizations to respond swiftly to changes and disruptions. For example, during the COVID-19 pandemic, many companies faced unprecedented challenges due to supply chain disruptions.

Organizations that had implemented real-time data collection mechanisms were better equipped to adapt their operations and respond to shifting consumer demands. The ability to track the status of shipments, monitor inventory levels, and analyze market trends in real time is crucial for maintaining agility in the logistics.

Furthermore, the rise of edge computing augments data collection efforts by allowing processing at or near the point of data production. Edge computing minimizes latency and bandwidth consumption, allowing enterprises to evaluate sensor data in real time rather than sending it all to a central server. This capacity is especially useful in contexts where rapid decision-making is required, such as manufacturing facilities or warehouses. Organizations can optimize processes and respond to anomalies with greater speed by processing data at the edge.

As businesses continue to explore the potential of sensors and APIs for data collection, collaboration with technology partners and stakeholders across the supply chain is essential. Establishing data-sharing agreements and fostering an ecosystem of trusted partners can enhance the richness and accuracy of the data collected. Collaborative data initiatives allow organizations to combine insights from different players in the supply chain, leading to more comprehensive analyses and informed decision-making. In addition, organizations should prioritize the development of a data-driven culture. This involves training employees to understand the value of data and empowering them to leverage insights in their daily operations. By fostering a culture that values data-driven decision-making, organizations can unlock the full potential of the information collected through sensors and APIs.

In summary, the introduction of sensors and APIs has altered data collecting in logistics, giving organizations the tools they need to improve visibility, responsiveness, and strategic decision-making. The integration of IoT devices allows for real-time monitoring, while APIs simplify data interchange across platforms. However, obstacles such as data volume, security, and compliance must be overcome before these technologies can be properly utilized. Organizations may enhance logistics operations and achieve long-term success in an increasingly competitive climate by investing in data management solutions, embracing advanced analytics, and cultivating a collaborative and data-driven culture.

Real-time data analytics and execution

Real-time data processing refers to the immediate handling of data as it is generated, enabling organizations to derive insights and act without delays. The advent of edge computing has significantly enhanced the capacity for real-time data processing by enabling data to be processed closer to its source, thereby reducing latency and bandwidth usage. According to a report by Gartner, edge computing is projected to account for nearly 75% of enterprise-generated data by 2025, highlighting its critical role in modern data architectures (Gartner, 2021). This shift is particularly relevant in logistics, where timely access to data can drive more effective decision-making and operational agility. The data value chain is illustrated in Figure 8.

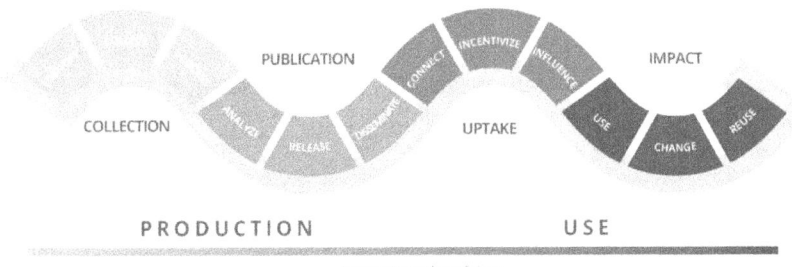

Figure 8 Data value chain[7]

Demand forecasting is one of the most common applications of real-time data processing in logistics. Traditional forecasting methods often rely on historical data and are slow to respond to rapid changes in consumer behavior or market conditions. In contrast, real-time data processing allows businesses to incorporate current sales data, social media trends, and external factors like weather conditions into their forecasting models. According to McKinsey & Company, organizations that use advanced analytics for demand forecasting can reduce forecasting errors by up to 50%. This increased accuracy not only improves inventory levels but also ensures that products are available when and where customers need them. Another critical area where real-time data processing has a significant impact is logistics visibility. Real-time tracking of shipments and inventory levels enables organizations to monitor goods throughout the supply chain, from production to delivery. For example, the use of GPS and RFID technologies allows businesses to track the location and status of shipments in real-time. According to a survey by the American Production and Inventory

---

[7] Adapted from data2x, https://opendatawatch.com/wp-content/uploads/Data-Value-Chain/ODW-Data2x-Data-Value-Chain-simple-CC-BY-ATTRIBUTION.jpg, CC BY-NC 2.0

Control Society (APICS), organizations with high visibility in their logistics experience 20% lower operational costs and 15% higher customer satisfaction. By leveraging real-time data, companies can proactively address potential disruptions, optimize routing, and improve service levels.

In addition to demand forecasting and visibility, real-time data processing also enhances operational planning and execution. For instance, manufacturers can utilize real-time data from production lines to adjust schedules, optimize resource allocation, and minimize downtime. By employing predictive analytics, organizations can identify potential equipment failures before they occur, allowing for timely maintenance and reducing the risk of production delays. A study by the International Data Corporation (IDC) found that organizations implementing predictive maintenance strategies can reduce maintenance costs by 10-40% and increase asset uptime by 5-10%. This proactive approach to asset management not only improves operational efficiency but also extends the lifespan of critical equipment.

The integration of real-time data processing in logistics management also facilitates agile decision-making. In uncertain and rapidly changing environments, organizations must be able to pivot quickly in response to new information. Real-time analytics tools enable decision-makers to access up-to-date information and insights, allowing them to adjust strategies, redistribute resources, or alter production schedules as needed. According to a survey by Deloitte, 62% of executives believe that real-time analytics will be crucial for their organizations to remain competitive over the next few years. This underscores the growing recognition of the need for agility in logistics operations.

However, implementing real-time data processing presents several challenges. One primary challenge is data integration. Logistics typically involve multiple stakeholders, each with their own systems and data formats. To achieve effective real-time data processing, organizations must integrate data from various sources, including suppliers, logistics providers, and internal systems. This often requires adopting advanced data integration solutions and standards to ensure compatibility and interoperability. Another issue is managing data quality. Real-time data processing heavily relies on the accuracy and reliability of incoming data. Incomplete or inaccurate data can lead to poor decisions and operational inefficiencies. Organizations must employ robust data governance methods, such as data validation, cleansing, and monitoring, to ensure high-quality data. Experian reported that poor data quality costs firms an average of $15 million per year. Thus, investing in data quality control is critical for reaping the full benefits of real-time data processing. Additionally, organizations must consider the security implications of real-time data processing. The increased connectivity of devices and systems within the logistics can expose organizations to cyber risks. According to the Cybersecurity & Infrastructure Security Agency (CISA), the frequency of cyberattacks on logistics has increased by 300% in recent years. Implementing strong security measures is essential to protect data and maintain trust.

To further illustrate the impact of sensors and APIs on data collection in logistics, consider the case of a leading global manufacturer that implemented a comprehensive IoT solution. By installing sensors on machinery and throughout their production facilities, the manufacturer was able to monitor equipment performance and production levels in real-time. This data was then transmitted via APIs to a centralized dashboard, where it could be analyzed for predictive maintenance and operational insights. The result was a significant reduction in downtime, increased efficiency, and lower operational costs. According to the company, they achieved a 15% increase in overall equipment effectiveness (OEE) within the first six months of deploying the IoT solution (Siemens, 2021). Additionally, retailers have begun leveraging sensors and APIs to enhance their inventory management processes. By utilizing RFID (Radio-Frequency Identification) tags on products, retailers can automatically track stock levels in real-time. This capability not only streamlines inventory management but also provides valuable insights into customer purchasing patterns, allowing for more accurate demand forecasting. A study found that RFID technology can reduce inventory shrinkage by as much as 50% and improve inventory accuracy to over 95% (Hardgrave et al., 2009). The ability to collect and analyze data through sensors and APIs empowers retailers to optimize their logistics and meet customer demands more effectively.

Moreover, the combination of cloud computing, IoT, and APIs enhances data collection capabilities by providing scalable storage and processing power. Cloud platforms enable businesses to store vast amounts of data collected from sensors without the limitations of traditional on-premises systems. As the volume of data generated by IoT devices increases, scalability becomes increasingly crucial. For instance, Cisco estimates that global IP traffic will exceed 4.8 zettabytes per year by 2022, driven largely by the growth of IoT devices. Cloud-based solutions facilitate real-time data processing and analysis, allowing enterprises to quickly derive actionable insights.

In addition to operational benefits, using sensors and APIs for data collection supports sustainability initiatives within logistics. By monitoring energy consumption, waste levels, and resource usage, organizations can identify areas for improvement and implement sustainable practices. For example, smart sensors can track energy usage in warehouses, enabling companies to optimize lighting and heating systems, thereby reducing their carbon footprint. According to a report by the Carbon Trust, organizations can achieve energy savings of up to 20% by utilizing IoT technology for energy management. This alignment of data collection with sustainability goals not only benefits the environment but also enhances corporate reputation and customer loyalty.

In conclusion, data collection through sensors and APIs is transforming logistics by providing organizations with real-time visibility, improved operational efficiency, and enhanced decision-making capabilities. The integration of IoT technologies facilitates the monitoring of key metrics, while APIs enable seamless data exchange across systems. However, organizations must address challenges related to data management, security, and compliance to fully leverage these innovations. By adopting best practices for data collection and investing in robust data management solutions, businesses can position themselves for success in an increasingly data-driven logistics landscape.

Privacy protection and data security

As logistics become increasingly interconnected and reliant on data-driven technologies, the importance of data security and privacy protection cannot be overstated. With the integration of

IoT devices and edge computing in logistics, vast amounts of sensitive data are generated and transmitted, making organizations vulnerable to cyber threats and privacy breaches. This section delves into the critical aspects of data security and privacy protection within the context of logistics management, exploring the threats, best practices, regulatory compliance, and the role of emerging technologies.

One of the primary threats to data security in logistics is the rise of cyberattacks targeting interconnected systems. According to the Cybersecurity & Infrastructure Security Agency (CISA), logistics are among the most targeted sectors, with a significant increase in ransomware attacks and data breaches in recent years (CISA, 2022). For instance, the SolarWinds cyberattack in 2020 exemplified how vulnerabilities in third-party software could compromise entire logistics, affecting thousands of organizations globally. This attack underscored the need for robust security measures, as organizations must ensure not just their own security but also that of their partners in the supply chain.

To mitigate these risks, organizations must adopt a multi-layered security approach that includes comprehensive risk assessments, encryption, access control, and continuous monitoring. Risk assessments allow organizations to identify potential vulnerabilities within their systems and logistics processes. By understanding their threat landscape, companies can prioritize security investments and implement measures to protect sensitive data. The National Institute of Standards and Technology (NIST) recommends conducting regular risk assessments as part of a proactive cybersecurity strategy (NIST, 2018).

Encryption is another fundamental element of data security. It ensures that data is rendered unreadable to unauthorized users, both during transmission and at rest. According to a report by the Ponemon Institute, organizations that employ encryption can reduce the average cost of a data breach by more than $1.4 million (Ponemon Institute, 2021). In logistics, where data is often transmitted across various networks and devices, encryption serves as a critical safeguard, protecting sensitive information from interception and unauthorized access. Organizations should implement strong encryption protocols, such as Advanced Encryption Standard (AES) and Transport Layer Security (TLS), to secure their data communications.

Access control techniques are essential to ensure that sensitive information is only accessed by authorized individuals. Role-based access control (RBAC) is a popular method that assigns access based on the specific roles and responsibilities of individuals within an organization. By restricting access to sensitive data to those who have a legitimate need to know, organizations can reduce the risk of insider threats and data leaks. According to an IBM analysis, roughly 95% of data breaches are caused by insider threats and human error (IBM, 2024). Regular access reviews, in conjunction with RBAC implementation, can significantly enhance data security.

An effective data security plan must encompass both threat detection and continuous monitoring. Organizations should utilize Security Information and Event Management (SIEM) systems to collect and analyze security data in real-time from across their networks. These systems can detect anomalies and potential threats, enabling swift responses to security incidents. According to an study, Aberdeen Group (2021), organizations that implement continuous monitoring are 30% more likely to detect a breach within the first 24 hours. Prompt detection is crucial for minimizing the impact of a data breach on logistics operations.

In addition to technical measures, regulatory compliance is a critical aspect of data security and privacy protection. Organizations must navigate a complex landscape of data protection regulations, such as the General Data Protection Regulation (GDPR) in the European Union and the California Consumer Privacy Act (CCPA) in the United States. Non-compliance with these regulations can result in severe penalties, including fines that can reach millions of dollars. According to a report by the International Association of Privacy Professionals (IAPP, 2021), the average cost of non-compliance with GDPR is estimated to be around €4.5 million. Organizations should establish comprehensive data governance frameworks to ensure compliance with applicable regulations, including data handling, consent management, and data subject rights.

Furthermore, privacy protection is increasingly becoming a concern for consumers and stakeholders. As organizations collect vast amounts of personal and sensitive data, transparency in data practices is essential to build trust. A study by PwC (2021) found that 79% of consumers are concerned about how companies use their personal data, and 85% would cease doing business with a company that violates their trust. To address these concerns, organizations should implement clear privacy policies, communicate data practices to customers, and provide options for data consent and opt-out mechanisms. The role of emerging technologies in enhancing data security and privacy cannot be overlooked. Blockchain technology, for instance, offers a decentralized and tamper-proof method of recording transactions and data exchanges. By leveraging blockchain, organizations can enhance the traceability and security of their data, transforming it into a strategic asset that drives competitive advantage in the logistics landscape.

In addition to the operational efficiencies gained through real-time data collection, organizations can leverage advanced analytics and machine learning algorithms to derive deeper insights from the data gathered by sensors and APIs. Predictive analytics, for example, can be employed to forecast demand fluctuations, enabling businesses to optimize inventory levels and minimize waste. A study by McKinsey & Company (2021) found that companies using advanced analytics in their logistics can achieve a 20-30% reduction in inventory costs while improving service levels. This demonstrates the substantial impact that effective data collection and analysis can have on overall logistics performance.

Furthermore, the integration of sensors and APIs fosters a more collaborative environment among logistics partners. By sharing real-time data across the logistics network, organizations can enhance responsiveness and coordination, reduce lead times, and increase customer satisfaction. For instance, when suppliers and manufacturers have access to real-time inventory levels and demand forecasts, they can better synchronize their operations, leading to smoother workflows and fewer bottlenecks. A collaborative approach to data sharing can result in more agile logistics operations that can quickly adapt to market changes.

Advancements in edge computing are also crucial for enhancing logistics data collection. Unlike relying solely on centralized cloud systems, edge computing allows data processing to occur closer to the location where the data is generated. This reduces latency and accelerates decision-making, which is particularly beneficial for logistics that require immediate insights from sensor data. For example, edge computing can facilitate real-time monitoring of equipment performance in a manufacturing setting, enabling predictive maintenance to minimize downtime and improve production processes. Gartner (2021) predicts that by 2025, at least 75% of enterprise-generated data will be created and processed outside of a traditional centralized data center or cloud. This shift towards edge computing underscores the need for organizations to rethink their data collection strategies. As organizations explore the potential of edge computing in data collection, they must also consider the implications for data governance and management. With data being processed at multiple points across the logistics network, establishing clear governance frameworks becomes essential to ensure data integrity, security, and compliance. Organizations should develop policies that outline data ownership, access rights, and accountability to mitigate risks associated with decentralized data processing.

In conclusion, the incorporation of sensors and APIs is transforming logistics by changing the methods for gathering, evaluating, and utilizing data. Real-time data collection from IoT devices enhances responsiveness and visibility, while APIs facilitate seamless data transfer between systems. To fully reap the benefits of these technologies, enterprises must address challenges related to data volume, integration, security, and compliance. By adopting a comprehensive approach to data collection that includes investments in advanced analytics, collaboration with logistics partners, and the use of edge computing, businesses can establish a data-driven culture that enhances operational efficiency and drives strategic decision-making. Ultimately, the success of logistics in the digital era depends on the ability to ethically and effectively leverage data.

References:

American Transportation Research Institute. (2021). Improving the efficiency of freight movement. Retrieved from https://truckingresearch.org/2021/03/15/improving-the-efficiency-of-freight-movement/

APICS. (2019). Supply chain visibility: Enhancing efficiency and customer satisfaction. Retrieved from https://forceget.com/blog/supply-chain-visibility-enhancing-efficiency-and-customer-satisfaction

Aberdeen Group. (2021). Continuous monitoring: The key to early breach detection. Retrieved from https://secureframe.com/blog/continuous-monitoring-cybersecurity

Carbon Trust. (2019). Digital technologies for energy management. Retrieved from https://www.carbontrust.com/our-work-and-impact/guides-reports-and-tools/digital-technologies-for-energy-management

Cisco. (2020). Cisco Annual Internet Report (2018–2023) White Paper. Retrieved from https://www.cisco.com/c/en/us/solutions/collateral/executive-perspectives/annual-internet-report/white-paper-c11-741490.html

Cybersecurity & Infrastructure Security Agency. (2022). 2021 trends show increased globalized threat of ransomware. Retrieved from https://www.cisa.gov/news-events/cybersecurity-advisories/aa22-040a

Deloitte. (2021). Building a competitive advantage through analytics. Retrieved from https://www2.deloitte.com/content/dam/Deloitte/nl/Documents/technology/deloitte-nl-strategy-building-a-competitive-advantage-through-analytics.pdf

Experian. (2021). The impact of poor data quality for a business. Retrieved from https://www.experianplc.com/newsroom/press-releases/2022/quality-data-proves-critical-to-business-performance

Gartner. (2021). What edge computing means for infrastructure and operations leaders. Retrieved from https://www.gartner.com/smarterwithgartner/what-edge-computing-means-for-infrastructure-and-operations-leaders

Hardgrave, B. C., Aloysius, J., & Goyal, S. (2009). Does RFID improve inventory accuracy? A preliminary analysis. *International Journal of RF Technologies, 1*(1), 44-56.

IBM. (2024). Cost of a Data Breach Report. Retrieved from https://www.ibm.com/security/data-breach

IDC. (2020). Predictive and prescriptive maintenance applications vital to asset life-cycle management software users. Retrieved from https://www.idc.com/getdoc.jsp?containerId=US50845423

International Association of Privacy Professionals. (2021). GDPR compliance and its financial impact. Retrieved from https://iapp.org/news/gdpr-compliance-costs

Li, B. (2009). Making a high-mix make-to-order production system lean. Master's dissertation, Massachusetts Institute of Technology.

Markets and Markets. (2020). IoT in supply chain market by component, application, and region - Global forecast to 2025. Retrieved from https://www.marketsandmarkets.com/Market-Reports/iot-in-supply-chain-market-129733727.html

McKinsey & Company. (2022). The impact of advanced analytics on supply chain performance. Retrieved from https://www.mckinsey.com/capabilities/operations/our-insights/a-more-resilient-supply-chain-from-optimized-operations-planning

MuleSoft. (2020). Connectivity benchmark report. Retrieved from https://www.mulesoft.com/lp/reports/connectivity-benchmark

National Institute of Standards and Technology. (2018). Risk management framework. Retrieved from https://csrc.nist.gov/Projects/Risk-Management

Ponemon Institute. (2021). Cost of a data breach report. Retrieved from https://www.ibm.com/reports/data-breach

PwC. (2021). Consumer trust and data privacy: Insights from the Global Consumer Insights Survey. Retrieved from https://www.pwc.com/gx/en/industries/consumer-markets/consumer-insights-survey.html

Siemens. (2021). Leverage IoT-based solutions for aerospace. Retrieved from https://resources.sw.siemens.com/en-US/e-book-aerospace-defense-leverage-iot-solutions

APPLICATIONS OF EDGE COMPUTING IN LOGISTICS

There are a variety of edge computing applications in logistics, and we review them in this chapter for each major logistics stage. For example, AWS Lambda@Edge is a feature of Amazon CloudFront that allows developers to run code closer to users, enhancing performance and reducing latency. It eliminates the need to manage infrastructure across multiple locations and supports various use cases and enables the creation of dynamic web applications that automatically scale without requiring origin infrastructure management (Amazon Web Services, 2024). As one example, users can personalize their experience by altering photos on the fly based on their unique traits. Photos can be resized according on the viewer's device type (mobile, desktop, or tablet). To increase image delivery performance, users can cache modified pictures at CloudFront Edge locations. The process for accomplishing this is illustrated in Figure 9.

According to IBM, key use cases of edge computing include optimizing business operations with AI and IoT data, improving performance in telecommunications, and enabling continuous operations across 5G networks. Edge computing supports real-time data analysis and decision-making, crucial for industries with high data volume and velocity (IBM, 2024). Techopedia discusses six real-world edge computing use cases, emphasizing its role in enabling instantaneous data analysis and business insights. These use cases span various industries, including food and beverage, where edge computing ensures real-time visibility and control over production processes. Edge computing improves combat decision-making in the military by enabling real-time data processing and sharing between drones and fighter jets. By handling sensitive data locally, the technology also satisfies security requirements (Rosencrance, 2023).

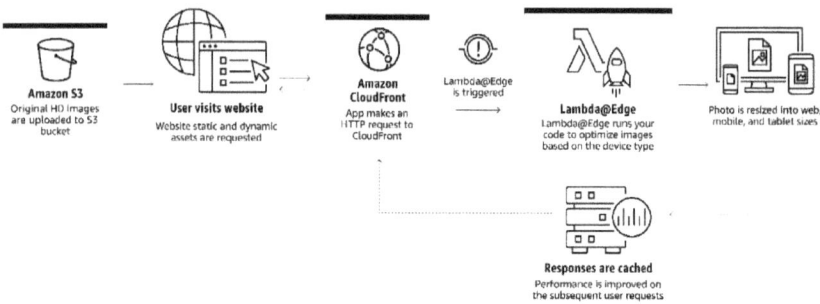

Figure 9 Image transformation with edge computing

Coordination with Supply Source

By facilitating real-time data processing and decision-making at the point of data generation, edge computing is transforming infrastructure and purchasing. To preserve efficiency and competitiveness in the face of the complex and dynamic character of modern logistics, it is imperative that this change be implemented.

Coordinating with supply sources, be it external suppliers or internal production facilities, is an essential part of logistics. Centralized data processing is a common component of traditional purchasing techniques, which can cause delays and inefficiencies. By decentralizing data processing, edge computing overcomes these difficulties and enables real-time analysis and decision-making at the network's edge (Zhang et al., 2024).

For instance, edge computing can enhance supplier management by providing real-time insights into supplier performance metrics such as delivery times, quality of goods, and compliance with contractual terms. By processing this data at the edge, companies can quickly identify and address issues, negotiate better terms, and optimize supplier relationships (Zhang et al., 2024). Additionally, edge computing enables predictive analytics, allowing purchasing managers to anticipate demand fluctuations and adjust purchasing strategies accordingly (Zhang et al., 2024). As another example, in the organic agricultural logistics, blockchain and edge computing can work together to provide real-time verification of product authenticity and compliance with organic standards (Hu et al., 2021). This integration helps build trust among stakeholders and ensures the integrity of the supply chain. In addition, AI may be used in purchasing to write contracts and get price quotes, which will save a lot of labor (Cui et al., 2022). Furthermore, by continuously learning, reasoning, making decisions, and acting to influence business results, AI can provide smarter control rules (Cui et al., 2022).

Case study of Grupo Pinsa

practical example of edge computing in purchasing and infrastructure optimization is the case of Grupo Pinsa, a leading tuna producer in Mexico. Grupo Pinsa implemented edge computing solutions to enhance its operations. By deploying edge devices across its facilities, Grupo Pinsa was able to ensure timely and accurate data on supplier performance and inventory levels by successfully monitoring and managing its purchasing operations

(Lenovo, 2024). For example, advanced sensors can monitor environmental conditions in real-time, ensuring that perishable goods are stored and transported under optimal conditions. Grupo Pinsa was able to optimize its purchasing strategy, lower expenses, and increase the overall efficiency of the supply chain thanks to this real-time data (Lenovo, 2024).

Digital Infrastructure

Infrastructure within the supply chain encompasses the physical and digital assets required to support purchasing, production, and distribution activities. Edge computing plays a critical role in the efficient use of these assets by supporting real-time monitoring and optimization. For example, edge devices can be deployed in warehouses and distribution centers to monitor environmental conditions, equipment performance, and inventory levels (Zhang et al., 2024). Proactive maintenance is made possible by this real-time data, which decreases downtime and increases the life of vital infrastructure. Furthermore, integration of Internet of Things (IoT) devices—which are being utilized more and more in logistics infrastructure—is made easier by edge computing. Large volumes of data are produced by IoT devices, and for them to be meaningful, they must be swiftly processed and analyzed. To ensure that data from IoT devices is processed in real-time and improve logistics operations' efficiency and responsiveness, edge computing supplies the required computational capacity at the network's edge (Zhang et al., 2024).

Case study of Gecko

Akamai's recent launch of its Generalized Edge Compute platform, Gecko, exemplifies the potential of edge computing in optimizing infrastructure. Gecko moves compute workloads that typically reside in centralized data centers to hard-to-reach edge locations, bringing full-stack computing closer to users (Teal, 2024). This shift allows for more efficient processing and faster response times, which are crucial for real-time decision-making in purchasing and other logistics activities. By integrating compute capabilities into its edge network, Akamai is addressing the growing demand for distributed cloud services (Teal, 2024).

While the benefits of edge computing in purchasing and infrastructure are significant, there are also challenges to consider. One of the primary challenges is data security. Processing data at several locations is a feature of edge computing, which raises the possibility of assaults and data breaches (Zhang et al., 2024). Businesses need to put strong security measures in place, such as encryption, access controls, and frequent security audits, to reduce these risks (Zhang et al., 2024). Integrating edge computing with current logistics systems presents another difficulty. A shift to a decentralized edge computing architecture might be difficult and expensive for businesses that have made significant investments in centralized data processing infrastructure (Zhang et al., 2024). To guarantee a seamless transition, thorough planning, investments in new technologies, and employee training are necessary.

In conclusion, edge computing is transforming the digital infrastructure of logistics by enabling real-time data processing and decision-making. With this transformation, the future of edge computing in this area looks promising, with emerging trends such as AI and ML poised to further enhance its impact.

Process optimization

Edge computing is changing the landscape of production and manufacturing by allowing for real-time data processing and decision-making at the point of data generation. This skill is critical for streamlining production processes, enhancing scheduling, and increasing operational efficiency. Traditional manufacturing systems often rely on centralized data processing, which can lead to latency issues and delays in decision-making. Edge computing addresses these challenges by decentralizing data processing, allowing for instantaneous analysis and feedback at the edge of the network. This capability is particularly beneficial in production environments where timely decisions are critical for maintaining efficiency and quality.

Edge computing, for example, can be used to monitor and analyze data from multiple sensors implanted in the production line while producing complex items like vehicles or electronics. This real-time data can be utilized to identify anomalies, predict equipment breakdowns, and optimize production schedules, minimizing downtime and increasing overall productivity (Kubiak et al., 2022). Furthermore, edge computing allows manufacturers to apply predictive maintenance plans, which can drastically reduce maintenance costs and increase the lifespan of essential equipment (Red Hat, 2023). Furthermore, edge computing enables the integration of AI and machine learning algorithms, which can analyze massive volumes of data to detect patterns and trends. This information can be utilized to optimize production schedules, eliminate waste, and increase resource use. For example, a hybrid industrial scheduling model based on collaborative edge computing can greatly reduce dynamic scheduling time while achieving real-time scheduling, improving overall production efficiency (Pan et al., 2022).

Case study of Tyson Foods

Tyson Foods, a leading food processing company, provides a compelling example of how edge computing can optimize production processes. The company has implemented edge computing solutions to collect and analyze data from its production lines in real-time. This data-driven approach enables Tyson Foods to monitor production parameters, detect anomalies, and optimize processes, resulting in improved product quality and operational efficiency (Google Cloud, 2023). By leveraging edge computing, Tyson Foods has transformed its production processes, turning data into valuable insights that drive continuous improvement.

While the advantages of edge computing in production and manufacturing are great, there are certain drawbacks to consider. One of the most significant challenges is data security. Edge computing includes processing data in various locations, increasing the danger of data breaches and cyberattacks. To reduce these risks, manufacturers must install strong security measures like as encryption, access controls, and frequent security audits (Kubiak et al., 2022). Another challenge is integrating edge computing into existing production systems. Many manufacturers have made significant investments in centralized data processing infrastructure, and switching to a decentralized edge computing architecture can be difficult and expensive. To guarantee a smooth transition, careful planning, investment in new technologies, and employee training are required (Red Hat, 2023).

The future of edge computing in production and manufacturing looks promising, with several emerging trends poised to further enhance its impact. One such trend is the increasing use of AI and ML at the edge. AI and ML algorithms can analyze data in real-time, providing valuable insights and automating decision-making processes. This capability is particularly useful in manufacturing, where AI and ML can help identify patterns, predict demand, and optimize production strategies (Pan et al., 2022). The creation of increasingly sophisticated edge devices and sensors is another trend. Manufacturing applications are becoming more complex as a result of these devices' increasing power and capacity to handle greater amounts of data. To ensure that items are made under ideal conditions, for instance, sophisticated sensors can track environmental conditions in real-time (Kubiak et al., 2022).

Warehousing and inventory tracking

Because edge computing allows for real-time data processing and decision-making at the point of data generation, it is changing inventory management and warehousing. The improvement of logistics performance overall, cost reduction, and operational efficiency all depend on this shift. Smart warehouses are evolving due to the combination of edge computing with other cutting-edge technologies like machine learning, artificial intelligence, and the Internet of Things (IoT).

The potential of edge computing to provide real-time inventory tracking is one of the main benefits for warehousing. The centralized data processing that is frequently the foundation of traditional inventory management systems can cause latency problems and delays in the updating of inventory information. By decentralizing data processing, edge computing provides fast updates and real-time visibility into inventory levels, thereby addressing these difficulties (NEC, 2017). This feature is especially helpful in dynamic warehouse environments where stockouts and overstock issues can be avoided, and ideal inventory levels can be maintained with timely information. For instance, by analyzing data from Internet of Things sensors mounted on shelves and bins, edge computing can be used to track inventory levels in real-time. Warehouse managers may make educated judgments about order fulfillment and restocking by using this data's ability to be instantly examined at the edge to provide insights into inventory status (NEC, 2017). Furthermore, real-time inventory tracking can increase the accuracy of inventory records and lower the possibility of human error, which will improve warehouse operations efficiency (NEC, 2017). An example of technology used for inventory tracking is provided in Figure 10.

Figure 10 Barcode that facilitates inventory tracking[8]

---

[8] Source: https://live.staticflickr.com/5164/5210268694_7a5a1ced08_z.jpg, CC BY-NC

By enabling real-time process monitoring and control, edge computing improves warehouse operations. Warehouses can decrease downtime and increase overall efficiency by promptly identifying and resolving operational issues by processing data at the edge. Edge computing, for example, can be used to track the efficiency of warehouse machinery like forklifts, conveyor belts, and automated storage and retrieval systems (AS/RS). By analyzing this real-time data, abnormalities and equipment failures can be predicted, enabling proactive maintenance and lowering the likelihood of unplanned malfunctions (Forbes, 2023). The integration of AI and ML algorithms, which can analyze enormous volumes of data to optimize warehouse operations, is also made easier by edge computing. AI-enabled edge devices, for instance, can be used to improve the arrangement of things in the warehouse, making sure that items that are frequently accessed are kept in easily accessible places. This can drastically cut down on the time and effort needed for picking and packing tasks, improving customer happiness and expediting order fulfillment (Forbes, 2023).

An essential component of efficient warehouse management is accurate inventory. Stockouts, overstock scenarios, and higher operating costs might result from inaccurate inventory records. Because edge computing allows real-time data processing and lessens the need for human data entry, it increases inventory accuracy. For example, by utilizing RFID technology and Internet of Things sensors, edge computing can be used to automate the inventory counting process. These sensors can reduce the possibility of human error and guarantee that inventory data is always current by continuously monitoring inventory levels and updating records in real-time (Ran, 2021). Furthermore, by offering real-time insights into inventory trends and demand patterns, edge computing can improve the accuracy of inventory forecasts. Warehouse managers can optimize inventory levels and lower the danger of stockouts or overstock situations by using edge computing to analyze historical data and current inventory levels to help them estimate future demand more accurately (Ran, 2021).

Case study of Wendy's

Wendy's, a leading fast-food chain, provides a compelling example of how edge computing can optimize warehousing and inventory management. The company has implemented edge computing solutions to collect and analyze data from its logistics operations in real-time. This data-driven approach enables Wendy's to monitor inventory levels, detect anomalies, and optimize processes, resulting in improved operational efficiency and reduced costs (Wendy's, 2023). By leveraging edge computing, Wendy's has transformed its retail operations, turning data into valuable insights that drive continuous improvement (Wendy's, 2023).

While the benefits of edge computing in warehousing and inventory management are significant, there are also challenges to consider. One of the primary challenges is data security. Edge computing involves processing data at multiple locations, which can increase the risk of data breaches and cyberattacks. To mitigate these risks, warehouses must implement robust security measures, including encryption, access controls, and regular security audits (NEC, 2017). Another challenge is the integration of edge computing with existing warehouse management systems. Many warehouses have invested heavily in centralized data processing infrastructure, and transitioning to a decentralized edge computing model can be complex and costly. It requires careful planning, investment in new technologies, and training for staff to ensure a smooth transition (NEC, 2017).

With a number of new trends poised to further enhance its impact, edge computing in inventory management and warehousing appears to have a bright future. The creation of increasingly sophisticated edge devices and sensors is another trend. More advanced warehousing applications are made possible by the increasing power and data processing capacity of these devices. To ensure that perishable commodities are stored and transported under ideal circumstances, for instance, sophisticated sensors can track environmental conditions in real-time (NEC, 2017).

Logistics and transportation optimization

Transportation optimization is essential to the dynamic world of logistics because they guarantee the smooth flow of goods from suppliers to consumers. The way logistics function has been completely transformed by the incorporation of edge computing technologies into logistics and transportation systems. These technologies provide increased efficiency, real-time data processing, and better decision-making capabilities. This section explores the use of edge computing in logistics and transportation optimization, emphasizing how it affects logistics performance overall, fleet management, route planning, and real-time tracking.

One of the primary applications of edge computing in logistics is in route planning and optimization. Traditional route planning methods often rely on centralized systems that may not provide real-time updates or adapt quickly to changing conditions. Edge computing, however, enables decentralized data processing at the edge of the network, allowing for real-time analysis of traffic conditions, weather patterns, and other variables that can affect transportation routes. This decentralized approach ensures that logistics providers can dynamically adjust routes to avoid delays, reduce fuel consumption, and improve delivery times. For instance, the use of satellite edge computing can provide real-time data on traffic congestion and road conditions, enabling more efficient route planning and reducing transit times (Satsearch, 2023). Logistics and transportation operations must be optimized, and this requires effective fleet management. Edge computing makes it easier to manage and monitor fleet cars in real time, giving important information about maintenance requirements, fuel economy, and vehicle performance. Logistics businesses may anticipate maintenance needs, identify abnormalities, and maximize vehicle use by analyzing data at the edge instead of depending on centralized data centers. In addition to lowering maintenance expenses and downtime, this improves the transportation network's overall effectiveness. To guarantee that fleets run as efficiently as possible, mobile edge computing solutions, for instance, can be used to track driver behavior and vehicle health (Hewlett Packard Enterprise, 2023).

Real-time visibility and tracking are crucial elements of contemporary transportation and logistics systems. Edge computing makes it possible to gather and analyze data from a variety of sensors and Internet of things (IoT) devices mounted on cars and freight. Accurate and current information on the location, state, and status of shipments can be obtained by analyzing this data in real-time. By having more visibility, logistics companies can proactively handle possible problems like delays or temperature swings in perishable items, guaranteeing that the products arrive at their destinations in the best possible shape. Research has demonstrated that by cutting lead times and raising customer satisfaction, real-time tracking and visibility can greatly improve logistics performance (Zhang & Wang, 2022).

The integration of edge computing with predictive analytics empowers logistics providers to make data-driven decisions that optimize transportation operations. By analyzing historical data and real-time information, edge computing systems can predict demand patterns, identify potential disruptions, and recommend optimal transportation strategies. This proactive approach enables logistics companies to allocate resources more efficiently, reduce operational costs, and improve service levels. For instance, predictive analytics can help determine the best times for dispatching vehicles, optimizing load distribution, and minimizing empty miles (Smith & Lee, 2021). Concerns about data privacy and security in logistics and transportation are also addressed by edge computing. Sensitive data can be processed locally at the edge, minimizing the chance of illegal access and data breaches by keeping the information closer to its source. In the context of logistics, where it is crucial to protect customer data and proprietary information, this is especially crucial. Strong security features like encryption and access controls can be implemented by edge computing platforms to protect data during transit (Brown & Davis, 2020).

Edge computing's potential application in self-driving trucks represents a huge leap in logistics and transportation. Autonomous vehicles navigate and make real-time choices using a variety of sensors and cameras. Edge computing allows these vehicles to analyze data locally, lowering latency and improving response times. This is critical for operations like obstacle detection, route planning, and emergency braking. By analyzing data at the edge, autonomous vehicles can operate more safely and effectively, lowering the chance of accidents and increasing overall traffic flow (Biswas & Wang, 2023).

Edge computing also supports vehicle-to-everything (V2X) communication, which allows autonomous vehicles to interact with other vehicles, infrastructure, and pedestrians. This communication is essential for coordinating movements, avoiding collisions, and optimizing traffic management. The integration of edge computing with V2X technology enhances the capabilities of autonomous vehicles, making them a viable option for logistics and transportation (McKinsey & Company, 2023).

Case studies of FedEx and Kargo

Several real-world applications and case studies demonstrate the effectiveness of edge computing in logistics and transportation optimization. For example, the collaboration between Dell Technologies, FedEx, and Switch showcases the deployment of edge computing solutions to enhance logistics operations. By leveraging edge computing, FedEx has improved its package tracking capabilities, enabling real-time visibility and more accurate delivery estimates (FedEx Newsroom, 2023). Similarly, the use of edge computing in the Ducati Corse racing team has optimized logistics and transportation for their racing operations, ensuring that critical components are delivered on time and in optimal condition (Lenovo, 2023). Another notable example is Kargo, a logistics technology company that utilizes edge computing to automate shipping and receiving processes at loading docks. By processing data from computer vision systems and other sensors at the edge, Kargo can inspect freight for damage, verify shipments, and update inventory systems in real-time. This reduces processing times and improves the accuracy of logistics operations (Kargo, 2023).

Delivery to stores and homes

The delivery, often referred to as the "last mile," is the critical stage where goods are delivered from a transportation hub to the final delivery destination in retail stores and homes. This stage is crucial for customer satisfaction and loyalty, as it directly impacts the customer's experience with the brand. The integration of edge computing into delivery is poised to significantly enhance efficiency, reduce costs, and improve overall service quality, which is the focus of this section.

One of the most significant advantages of edge computing in last-mile delivery is the ability to track and view goods in real time. By processing data at the edge, logistics companies may provide clients with real-time information about the status and location of their delivery. This real-time visibility not only improves customer happiness by providing exact delivery times, but it also enables businesses to solve any difficulties that may develop during the delivery process. For example, edge computing can enable the use of IoT sensors and GPS tracking devices to monitor package condition and position, keeping customers informed of any delays or changes in delivery dates (CNBC, 2024). Edge computing plays a crucial role in optimizing delivery routes, which is essential for reducing delivery times and operational costs. Traditional route optimization methods often rely on centralized systems that may not be able to process real-time data efficiently. In contrast, edge computing allows for decentralized data processing, enabling logistics companies to analyze traffic conditions, weather patterns, and other variables in real-time. This real-time analysis allows for dynamic route adjustments, ensuring that delivery drivers can avoid traffic congestion and other obstacles, ultimately leading to faster and more efficient deliveries (Google Cloud, 2024).

Edge computing enables logistics companies to provide personalized and interactive customer experiences. For example, companies can use edge computing to send real-time notifications to customers about the status of their deliveries, including estimated arrival times and any potential delays. Additionally, edge computing can facilitate two-way communication between customers and delivery drivers, allowing customers to provide specific delivery instructions or request changes to their delivery windows. This level of engagement helps build trust and enhances the overall customer experience (Wavestone, 2024).

The integration of edge computing into last-mile delivery operations can significantly improve operational efficiency. By processing data locally, edge computing reduces the reliance on centralized data centers, leading to faster decision-making and reduced latency. This is particularly important for time-sensitive deliveries, such as perishable goods or medical supplies. Edge computing can also support the use of autonomous delivery vehicles and drones, which require real-time data processing to navigate and make decisions. These technologies can help reduce labor costs and increase delivery speed, further enhancing operational efficiency (Yang et al., 2020).

Case studies of Sensormatic and IBM

Several real-world applications and case studies demonstrate the effectiveness of edge computing in delivery. For instance, Sensormatic Solutions has leveraged edge computing to enhance the retail experience by providing real-time inventory visibility and optimizing store operations. This technology allows retailers to ensure that products are always available for customers, reducing the likelihood of stockouts and improving customer satisfaction (Lenovo, 2022). Another example is IBM's development of a custom edge computing solution for space, which highlights the versatility and scalability of edge computing technologies. This solution enables real-time data processing and analysis in remote and challenging environments, demonstrating the potential of edge computing to transform various industries, including logistics and supply chain management (IBM, 2023).

In conclusion, the integration of edge computing into last-mile delivery and customer service offers significant benefits for logistics optimization. By enabling real-time tracking and visibility, optimizing delivery routes, enhancing customer engagement, and improving operational efficiency, edge computing transforms last-mile delivery operations into more efficient and responsive systems. The adoption of edge computing in last-mile delivery not only reduces operational costs and enhances service levels but also ensures the security and privacy of sensitive data. As logistics continue to evolve, the role of edge computing in last-mile delivery and customer service will become increasingly critical, driving innovation and improving overall supply chain performance.

Autonomous vehicle

The integration of edge computing in autonomous vehicles (AVs) represents a significant advancement in the logistics sector, promising enhanced efficiency, safety, and reliability. Edge computing, by processing data closer to the source, reduces latency and bandwidth usage, which is crucial for the real-time decision-making required in autonomous driving. This section explores the multifaceted applications of edge computing in AVs, highlighting its impact on logistics processes.

The location of computing can be illustrated in Table 2.

Table 2 Computing in vehicles

On vehicle	Off vehicle, edge	Off vehicle, cloud
Emergency braking	Traffic management	Entertainment
Seat belt and airbag monitoring	Collision warning across lanes	Platooning
Collision warning (front and back)	Rare event monitoring	
Cooling management		

One of the primary benefits of edge computing in autonomous vehicles is the enhancement of real-time decision-making capabilities. Autonomous vehicles rely on a plethora of sensors and cameras to navigate and make split-second decisions. By processing this data at the edge, AVs can significantly reduce the time it takes to analyze and act on information. This is particularly important in logistics, where timely deliveries are critical. For instance, edge computing enables AVs to quickly adapt to changing traffic conditions, optimize routes, and avoid potential hazards, thereby ensuring efficient and safe transportation of goods (Analytics Steps, 2024).

Data security and privacy are paramount in the deployment of autonomous vehicles. Edge computing addresses these concerns by minimizing the amount of data transmitted to central servers. Instead, sensitive information is processed locally, reducing the risk of data breaches and ensuring compliance with privacy regulations. This localized data processing not only enhances security but also improves the overall reliability of AV systems. In logistics, where the protection of proprietary information and customer data is crucial, edge computing provides a robust solution (Arrow, 2024).

The reduction of latency and bandwidth usage is another significant advantage of edge computing in autonomous vehicles. Traditional cloud computing models require data to be sent to distant data centers for processing, which can introduce delays and consume substantial bandwidth. Edge computing, on the other hand, processes data closer to the vehicle, resulting in faster response times and reduced bandwidth requirements. This is particularly beneficial in logistics, where real-time data processing is essential for tasks such as route optimization, fleet management, and predictive maintenance (McKinsey & Company, 2024). This advantage of edge computing allows for Advanced Driver Assistance Systems (ADAS) and Vehicle-to-Everything (V2X). ADAS are critical components of autonomous vehicles, providing features such as collision avoidance, lane-keeping assistance, and adaptive cruise control. Edge computing enhances the performance of ADAS by enabling real-time data processing and analysis. This allows AVs to respond more quickly to dynamic driving conditions and improve overall safety. In the logistics sector, ADAS equipped with edge computing capabilities can help reduce accidents, lower insurance costs, and improve the reliability of delivery services (Ibn-Khedher et al., 2024). Using Integer Linear Programming (ILP) and deep reinforcement learning, AVs can solve the optimization problem and offload computing tasks to the network edge (Ibn-Khedher et al., 2024). V2X communication is a key technology that enables autonomous vehicles to interact with other vehicles, infrastructure, and pedestrians. Edge computing plays a crucial role in V2X communication by providing the necessary computational power and low-latency processing required for seamless interactions. This technology allows AVs to share real-time information about traffic conditions, road hazards, and optimal routes, thereby enhancing the efficiency and safety of logistics operations. For example, V2X communication can help AVs coordinate with traffic signals to reduce congestion and improve delivery times (We et al., 2021).

The integration of edge computing with Internet of Things (IoT) and Artificial Intelligence (AI) technologies further enhances the capabilities of autonomous vehicles. IoT devices provide a continuous stream of data from various sources, while AI algorithms analyze this data to make informed decisions. Edge computing enables the real-time processing of IoT data and the execution of AI models at the edge, resulting in faster and more accurate decision-making. In logistics, this integration allows for the seamless coordination of AVs with other smart devices and systems, improving overall operational efficiency. The integration with IoT and AI facilitates predictive maintenance, an essential aspect of fleet management in the logistics industry. By leveraging edge computing, autonomous vehicles can continuously monitor their own health and predict potential failures before they occur. This is achieved through the real-time analysis of data from various sensors and diagnostic tools. Predictive maintenance helps reduce downtime, extend the lifespan of vehicles, and lower maintenance costs. In logistics, where vehicle reliability is critical, edge computing provides a proactive approach to maintenance that ensures the smooth operation of AV fleets (Biswas & Wang, 2023).

Energy efficiency is a critical consideration for autonomous vehicles, particularly in the context of electric AVs. Edge computing contributes to energy efficiency by optimizing the processing power and reducing the need for constant communication with remote servers. This localized processing reduces the energy consumption associated with data transmission and cloud computing. In logistics, where fuel and energy costs are significant, the energy efficiency provided by edge computing can lead to substantial cost savings and a reduced environmental footprint.

Despite the numerous benefits, the implementation of edge computing in autonomous vehicles also presents several challenges. These include the need for robust edge infrastructure, the management of large volumes of data, and the development of standardized protocols for V2X communication. Additionally, ensuring the security and reliability of edge computing systems is critical to prevent potential cyber threats. Future research and development efforts should focus on addressing these challenges and exploring new opportunities for the integration of edge computing in AVs. This includes advancements in edge AI, the deployment of 5G networks, and the exploration of blockchain technology for secure data management.

In conclusion, edge computing plays a pivotal role in the advancement of autonomous vehicles, offering significant benefits in terms of real-time decision-making, data security, latency reduction, and energy efficiency. By integrating edge computing with IoT and AI technologies, AVs can achieve higher levels of performance and reliability, making them an invaluable asset in the logistics sector. As research and development continue to evolve, the future of autonomous vehicles in logistics looks promising, with edge computing at the forefront of this technological revolution.

References:

Amazon Web Services. (2024). Edge computing| CDN, global serverless code, distribution. Retrieved from https://aws.amazon.com/lambda/edge/?nc1=h_ls

Analytics Steps. (2024). The Future of Autonomous Cars with Edge Computing. Retrieved from https://www.analyticssteps.com/blogs/future-autonomous-cars-edge-computing

Arrow. (2024). Sensors and Edge AI: How They Work Together to Provide Autonomous Driving. Retrieved from https://www.arrow.com/en/research-and-events/articles/sensors-and-edge-ai-how-they-work-together-to-provide-autonomous-driving

Biswas, A., & Wang, H.-C. (2023). Autonomous vehicles enabled by the integration of IoT, edge intelligence, 5G, and blockchain. Sensors, 23(4), 1963. https://doi.org/10.3390/s23041963

Brown, A., & Davis, M. (2020). Security and data privacy in edge computing. Computer Security Journal, 39(2), 78-92. https://doi.org/10.1109/CSJ.2020.8339513

CNBC. (2024). Computing and storage are moving to the edge, and it needs to be ready. Retrieved from https://www.cnbc.com/2024/06/11/computing-and-storage-are-moving-to-the-edge-and-it-needs-to-be-ready.html

Cui, R., Li, M., & Zhang, S. (2022). AI and purchasing. Manufacturing & Service Operations Management, 24(2), 691-706.

Dave, D. M., & Mehta, R. (2024). Edge computing: Use cases in manufacturing and IoT. International Journal of Global Innovations and Solutions. Retrieved from https://ijgis.pubpub.org/pub/uuh6pipb/release/1

FedEx Newsroom. (2023). Dell Technologies, FedEx, and Switch team up to deliver exascale multi-cloud capabilities to the edge. Retrieved from https://newsroom.fedex.com/newsroom/united-states-english/dell-technologies-fedex-and-switch-team-up-to-deliver-exascale-multi-cloud-capabilities-to-the-edge

Google Cloud. (2024). Retail use cases for Google Distributed Cloud Edge. Retrieved from https://cloud.google.com/

blog/topics/hybrid-cloud/retail-use-cases-for-google-distributed-cloud-edge

Google Cloud. (2023). Tyson Foods turns chicken feed and filets into data riches. Google Cloud. Retrieved from https://cloud.google.com/transform/tyson-foods-turns-chicken-feed-and-filets-into-data-riches

Hewlett Packard Enterprise. (2023). What is mobile edge computing? Retrieved from https://www.hpe.com/fi/en/what-is/mobile-edge-computing.html

Hu, S., Huang, S., Huang, J., & Su, J. (2021). Blockchain and edge computing technology enabling organic agricultural supply chain: A framework solution to trust crisis. Computers & Industrial Engineering, 153, 107079. https://doi.org/10.1016/j.cie.2020.107079

IBM. (2024). Edge computing: Top use cases. Retrieved from https://www.ibm.com/topics/edge-computing-use-cases

IBM. (2023). IBM develops a unique custom edge computing solution in space. Retrieved from https://www.ibm.com/cloud/blog/ibm-develops-a-unique-custom-edge-computing-solution-in-space

Ibn-Khedher, H., Laroui, M., Mabrouk, M. B., Moungla, H., Afifi, H., Oleari, A. N., & Kamal, A. E. (2021). Edge Computing Assisted Autonomous Driving Using Artificial Intelligence. https://doi.org/10.1109/iwcmc51323.2021.9498627

Kargo. (2023). Edge computing in logistics: Everything you need to know. Retrieved from https://mykargo.com/blog/edge-computing-logistics

Kubiak, K., Dec, G., & Stadnicka, D. (2022). Possible applications of edge computing in the manufacturing industry—Systematic literature review. Sensors, 22(7), 2445. https://doi.org/10.3390/s22072445

Lenovo. (2023). Ducati Corse case study. Retrieved from https://www.lenovo.com/content/dam/lenovo/iso/customer-references-coe/global/en/case-studies/ducati-corse/lenovo_ducaticorse_casestudy.pdf

Lenovo. (2024). Grupo Pinsa case study. Retrieved from https://www.lenovo.com/content/dam/lenovo/iso/customer-references-coe/global/en/case-studies/grupo-pinsa/lenovo_grupopinsa_casestudy.pdf

Lenovo. (2022). Sensormatic Solutions leads a whole new retail experience. Retrieved from https://www.lenovo.com/content/dam/lenovo/iso/customer-references-coe/global/en/case-studies/sensormatic-solutions/Sensormatic%20Solutions%20leads%20a%20whole%20new%20retail%20experience.pdf

McKinsey & Company. (2024). The Future of Automotive Computing: Cloud and Edge. Retrieved from https://www.mckinsey.com/industries/semiconductors/our-insights/the-future-of-automotive-computing-cloud-and-edge

McKinsey & Company. (2023). Edge and cloud computing in the automotive industry. Retrieved from https://www.mckinsey.com/industries/semiconductors/our-insights/the-future-of-automotive-computing-cloud-and-edge

Pan, Z., Hou, X., Xu, H., Bao, L., & Jian, C. (2022). A hybrid manufacturing scheduling optimization strategy in collaborative edge computing. Evolutionary Intelligence, 17(1), 1065-1077. https://doi.org/10.1007/s12065-022-00786-z

Ran, H. (2021). Construction and optimization of inventory management system via cloud-edge collaborative computing in supply chain environment in the Internet of Things era. PloS One, 16(11), e0259284.

Red Hat. (2023). Edge computing in manufacturing. Red Hat. Retrieved from https://www.redhat.com/en/topics/edge-computing/manufacturing

Rosencrance, L. (2023). 6 real-world edge computing use cases. Techopedia. Retrieved from https://www.techopedia.com/6-real-world-edge-computing-use-cases

Satsearch. (2023). Satellite edge computing suppliers on the global market. Retrieved from https://blog.satsearch.co/2023-05-03-satellite-edge-computing-suppliers-on-the-global-market

Smith, J., & Lee, K. (2021). Predictive analytics in transportation optimization. International Journal of Logistics Management, 32(4), 123-140. https://doi.org/10.1002/cpe.6068

Teal, K. (2024). Akamai targets edge computing market with Gecko. Data Center Knowledge. Retrieved from https://www.datacenterknowledge.com/edge-data-centers/akamai-targets-edge-computing-market-with-gecko

Wavestone. (2024). Optimising operations efficiency and user experience with edge computing. Retrieved from https://wwa.wavestone.com/en/insight/optimising-operations-efficiency-and-user-experience-with-edge-computing/

Wu, Q., Xu, X., Zhao, Q., & Dai, F. (2021). Tasks offloading for connected autonomous vehicles in edge computing. Mobile Networks and Applications, 27(6), 2295–2304. https://doi.org/10.1007/s11036-021-01794-6

Yang, X., Han, M., Tang, H., Li, Q., & Luo, X. (2020). Detecting defects with support vector machine in logistics packaging boxes for edge computing. IEEE Access, 8, 64002-64010.

Zhang, X., Li, Y., & Wang, J. (2024). Edge computing in supply chain management: A comprehensive review. Journal of Cloud Computing, 13(1), 1-20. https://doi.org/10.1186/s13677-024-00626-8

Zhang, Y., & Wang, X. (2022). Real-time tracking and visibility in supply chain management. Journal of Supply Chain Management, 58(3), 45-60. https://doi.org/10.1155/2022/1823762

EMERGING LOGISTICS TECHNOLOGIES AND EDGE COMPUTING

In this chapter, we discuss several emerging technologies expected to contribute to supply chain management and how they can integrate with edge computing for greater gains.

Internet of Things (IoT) and edge computing

This section investigates the relationship between IoT and edge computing, highlighting their synergies, benefits, and limitations in the context of supply chain management.

The Internet of Things (IoT) has emerged as a disruptive force across industries, changing the way data is collected, processed, and used in supply chain management. By linking physical equipment to the internet, IoT enables real-time data sharing and communication, ultimately improving operational efficiency and decision-making. However, as the volume of data created by IoT devices grows, the constraints of standard cloud computing architectures become more apparent, necessitating the use of edge computing solutions. IoT devices, such as sensors, RFID tags, and smart machines, generate vast amounts of data that can provide valuable insights into logistics operations. According to a report by McKinsey, the economic potential of the IoT could reach up to $11 trillion by 2025, with significant contributions from supply chain improvements (McKinsey Global Institute, 2019). For example, temperature and humidity sensors in cold chain logistics can monitor the conditions of perishable goods in real-time, ensuring compliance with regulatory standards and reducing spoilage. The ability to collect and analyze data at the source enhances visibility and responsiveness, allowing organizations to make informed decisions based on current conditions.

However, the sheer volume of data created by IoT devices presents major hurdles to typical cloud computing platforms. Transmitting huge datasets to centralized cloud servers might result in latency concerns, increased bandwidth expenditures, and data loss. Edge computing tackles these difficulties by processing data closer to its source, decreasing the requirement for long-distance data transmission. The integration of the Internet of Things (IoT) and edge computing offers a big step forward in supply chain management, providing increased efficiency, real-time data processing, and better decision-making capabilities. IoT is a network of networked devices that gather and share data, whereas edge computing processes data closer to its source rather than using centralized cloud servers. This synergy between IoT and edge computing is transforming logistics by enabling faster and more reliable data processing, reducing latency, and enhancing operational efficiency.

One of the primary benefits of combining IoT with edge computing is the ability to process data in real-time. IoT devices generate vast amounts of data from various sources, such as sensors, RFID tags, and GPS trackers, which are crucial for monitoring and managing logistics operations. By processing this data at the edge, near the data source, organizations can achieve real-time insights and make immediate decisions. This is particularly important for applications such as predictive maintenance, inventory management, and demand forecasting, where timely data processing can significantly impact operational efficiency (Red Hat, 2022). According to a study by Nguyen et al. (2023), edge computing can reduce data processing time by up to 50%, leading to more responsive logistics operations. Edge computing minimizes the latency of data transfer to centralized cloud servers. In traditional cloud-based systems, data from IoT devices is sent to a central server for processing, which might cause delays. These delays are especially problematic in time-sensitive applications like driverless vehicles and real-time tracking systems. By processing data at the edge, organizations may reduce latency and ensure that key choices are made quickly. This is required to ensure the smooth flow of goods and services throughout the supply chain (PhoenixNAP, 2022). According to Statista (2024), the number of IoT devices globally is predicted to nearly quadruple, from 15.9 billion in 2023 to more than 32.1 billion by 2030, emphasizing the growing demand for efficient data processing solutions.

Security and privacy are significant concerns in supply chain management, particularly when dealing with sensitive information. IoT devices frequently collect and transmit data that may be vulnerable to intrusions. Edge computing improves security by processing data locally, eliminating the need to send sensitive information over potentially unsecured networks. This localized data processing reduces the danger of data breaches and guarantees that sensitive information is kept secure. Furthermore, edge computing can use advanced security methods such encryption and access management to protect data (IBM Developer, 2021). Hasan and Idrees (2024) argue that edge computing can dramatically minimize the attack surface by restricting the exposure of critical data to external threats.

The integration of IoT and edge computing significantly improves network bandwidth. IoT devices create huge amounts of data, which can strain network capacity when sent to a central server for processing. Edge computing reduces this strain by processing data locally and sending only relevant information to the cloud. This selective data transmission decreases the quantity of data that needs to be sent across the network, freeing up bandwidth for other vital processes. As a result, enterprises can use networks more efficiently and cost-effectively (Red Hat, 2022). According to Statista (2024), the worldwide edge computing market is expected to reach $350 billion by 2027, driven by the growing use of IoT devices and the demand for fast data processing.

Edge computing delivers the scalability and flexibility required to accommodate the increasing number of IoT devices in logistics. As the number of connected devices expands, so does the amount of data created, necessitating scalable data processing solutions. Edge computing enables enterprises to extend their data processing capacity by adding more edge devices as needed. This decentralized strategy assures that the system can handle greater data loads while maintaining performance. Furthermore, edge computing provides flexibility in deploying and administering IoT applications, allowing enterprises to react to changing business requirements (PhoenixNAP, 2022). The combination of IoT and edge computing has several applications in supply chain management. One significant application is predictive maintenance, in which IoT sensors monitor the health of equipment and machinery in real time. By evaluating this data at the edge, enterprises can discover possible problems before they cause equipment failure, lowering downtime and maintenance costs. Another use case is real-time inventory management, in which IoT sensors monitor the movement and status of commodities along the supply chain. Edge computing allows firms to optimize inventory levels and reduce stockouts by processing data immediately (IBM Developer, 2021). A study by Nguyen et al. (2023) discovered that edge computing can enhance inventory accuracy by up to 30%, resulting in more efficient logistics. An example of the typical setting of IoT application is provided in Figure 11.

Figure 11 Production floor is ripe for IoT applications[9]

Despite the obvious benefits, combining IoT and edge computing brings certain problems. One key problem is guaranteeing

---

[9] Source: https://www.constructionworld.in/assets/uploads/5ac1254df055bf0077a58440d3da762a.jpg. CC0 1.0 license

interoperability among various IoT devices and edge computing platforms. IoT data integration and processing might be complicated due to the wide range of devices and protocols used. Furthermore, controlling and maintaining many edge devices can be challenging and resource intensive. Organizations must invest in strong device management solutions to assure the stability and performance of their edge computing infrastructure. Furthermore, resolving security and privacy concerns necessitates ongoing monitoring and updating of security measures to protect against emerging threats (Red Hat, 2022).

In conclusion, the joint application of IoT and edge computing is revolutionizing supply chain management by enabling real-time data processing, reducing latency, enhancing security, and optimizing network bandwidth. This synergy offers significant benefits, including improved operational efficiency, scalability, and flexibility. However, organizations must also address the challenges associated with interoperability, device management, and security to fully leverage the potential of IoT and edge computing.

Robotics technology and edge computing

The convergence of robotics technology and computing represents a significant advancement in the landscape of logistics. As organizations strive for greater efficiency, flexibility, and responsiveness, the integration of these two technologies is enabling smarter, more autonomous systems that can operate effectively in complex environments. This section explores how robotics and edge computing synergize to enhance logistics operations.

Robotics technology has evolved rapidly over the past few decades, transitioning from traditional automated systems to increasingly sophisticated autonomous robots. These robots are now capable of performing a wide range of tasks, from warehouse management and inventory control to last-mile delivery. According to a report by the International Federation of Robotics, global sales of professional service robots, which include logistics and warehouse robots, increased by 32% in 2020, demonstrating a growing adoption of robotics in various sectors (International Federation of Robotics, 2021). As organizations increasingly rely on robotic solutions for operational tasks, the need for real-time data processing and analysis becomes paramount, which is where edge computing plays a vital role.

The integration of robotics technology with edge computing is revolutionizing supply chain management by enhancing automation, improving efficiency, and enabling real-time decision-making. Robotics technology encompasses a wide range of applications, including autonomous vehicles, robotic arms, and drones, all of which can benefit significantly from the capabilities of edge computing. This section explores the synergy between robotics and edge computing, highlighting key benefits, challenges, and future trends. Edge computing allows robots to process data locally, which eliminates the need for constant connectivity with centralized cloud servers. This local data processing capability is critical for applications that require low latency and immediate decision-making. For example, autonomous mobile robots (AMRs) employed in warehouses can navigate and complete jobs more effectively by analyzing sensor data at the edge. According to a study by Huang et al. (2022), edge computing can cut data processing delay in robotic systems by up to 39%, considerably improving operational efficiency.

One of the primary advantages of integrating edge computing with robotics is the ability to make real-time decisions, like IoT. Robots equipped with edge computing capabilities can analyze data from sensors and cameras instantaneously, allowing them to respond to dynamic environments quickly. This is particularly important for applications such as autonomous vehicles and drones, where real-time decision-making is critical for safety and performance. A report by Moon et al. (2024) highlights that edge computing can improve the responsiveness of autonomous driving systems by enabling real-time sharing of object information on roads.

Case Study: Autonomous Mobile Robots for Industry 4.0 Warehouses

In the rapidly evolving landscape of warehouse automation, Autonomous Mobile Robots (AMRs) have emerged as a pivotal technology. These robots, equipped with advanced sensors, cameras, and artificial intelligence, navigate autonomously within warehouse environments, enhancing efficiency and accuracy. A study by Grover and Ashraf (2024) explored the assimilation of AMRs in production warehouses. The research identified key moderating factors influencing the successful integration of AMRs, including organizational attributes of end-users, service attributes of providers, technology attributes of AMRs, and relational attributes between providers and end-users (Grover & Ashraf, 2024). Edge computing plays a crucial role in the deployment of AMRs by enabling real-time data processing and decision-making at the edge of the network. This reduces latency and enhances the robots' ability to respond swiftly to dynamic warehouse conditions. The study highlighted that edge computing allows AMRs to process vast amounts of data locally, improving operational efficiency and reducing dependency on centralized cloud infrastructure (Grover & Ashraf, 2024).

The integration of AMRs with edge computing resulted in significant improvements in productivity, reduced operating costs, and greater accuracy in inventory management. The study concluded that the successful assimilation of AMRs in warehouses is contingent upon a synergistic relationship between technology providers and end-users, facilitated by edge computing (Grover & Ashraf, 2024). The case study underscores the transformative potential of AMRs in warehouse automation, particularly when combined with edge computing. This integration not only enhances operational efficiency but also paves the way for more scalable and adaptable warehouse management solutions.

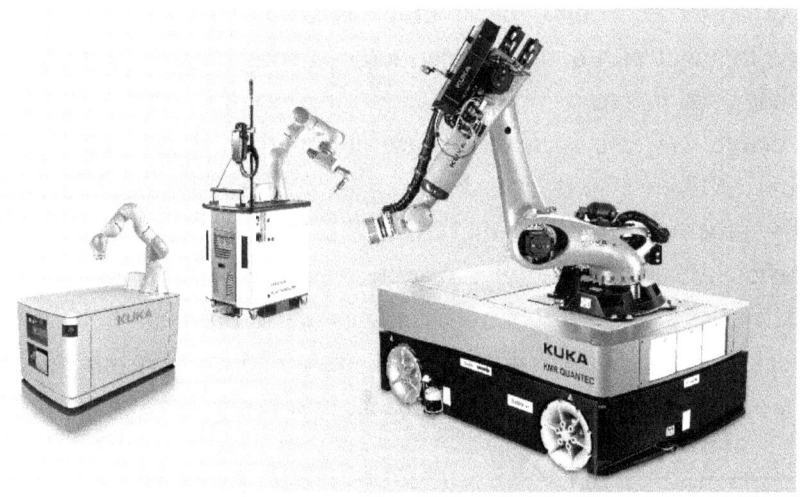

Figure 12 Mobile robots[10]

Edge computing enhances the reliability and resilience of robotic systems by reducing their dependence on cloud connectivity. In scenarios where network connectivity is unreliable or unavailable, robots can continue to operate effectively by processing data locally. This is particularly beneficial for logistics operations in remote or challenging environments. Additionally, edge computing allows for distributed data processing, which can improve the fault tolerance of robotic systems. If one edge node fails, others can take over its tasks, ensuring continuous operation.

The combination of robotics and edge computing provides tremendous scalability and flexibility in logistics operations. As the number of robots in a supply chain increases, so does the volume of data created. Edge computing is a scalable technology that allows data to be handled at numerous edge nodes, dispersing computational load. This decentralized strategy ensures that the system can handle higher data volumes while maintaining performance. Edge computing also facilitates the flexible deployment of robotic applications, allowing enterprises to react to changing business objectives and operational constraints. One notable use case is in warehouse automation, where robotic arms and AMRs are used for tasks, such as picking, packing, and sorting. By processing data at the edge, these robots can operate more efficiently and accurately. Another application is in logistics and delivery, where autonomous vehicles and drones can benefit from real-time data processing to navigate complex environments and optimize delivery routes. According to a report by Statista (2024),

---

[10] Source: Wikepedia Commons,
https://commons.wikimedia.org/wiki/File:Mobile_Robots_header.jpg, CC BY-SA 4.0

the global market for warehouse automation is expected to reach $30 billion by 2026, driven by advancements in robotics and edge computing. An example of mobile robots is provided in Figure 12.

Despite the numerous benefits, integrating robotics with edge computing also presents challenges. One significant challenge is ensuring interoperability between different robotic systems and edge computing platforms. The diverse range of devices and protocols used in robotics can complicate data integration and processing. Additionally, managing and maintaining many edge devices can be complex and resource intensive. Organizations must invest in robust device management solutions to ensure the reliability and performance of their edge computing infrastructure. Furthermore, addressing security and privacy concerns requires continuous monitoring and updating of security measures to protect against evolving threats.

The future of robotics and edge computing in supply chain management looks bright, with numerous new trends predicted to propel further progress. One such development is the use of artificial intelligence (AI) and machine learning (ML) with edge computing to improve the capabilities of robotic systems. AI and ML algorithms can be used at the edge to allow advanced features like predictive maintenance, anomaly detection, and autonomous decision-making. Another development is the deployment of 5G connection, which will enable the high-speed, low-latency communication required for real-time data processing and coordination across several robots. Seisa et al. (2022) found that combining 5G with edge computing can considerably improve robotic system performance and scalability.

To summarize, the merger of robotics technology with edge computing is altering supply chain management by increasing automation, improving efficiency, and enabling real-time decision-making. This synergy provides numerous advantages, including increased reliability, scalability, and adaptability. To fully realize the potential of robotics and edge computing, enterprises must handle obstacles such as interoperability, device management, and security. As technology advances, the integration of robotics and edge computing will become increasingly important in creating the future of supply chain management.

Generative AI and edge computing

The convergence of generative artificial intelligence (AI) and computing is a rapidly growing area of interest in supply chain management, with the potential to improve operational efficiency, decision-making, and creativity. Generative AI refers to algorithms that can generate new content, designs, or solutions from existing data, whereas edge computing processes data closer to the source rather than relying primarily on centralized data centers. These technologies can alter logistics processes by allowing for real-time data analysis, lowering latency, and maximizing resource use. This section investigates the relationship between generative AI and edge computing, exploring its applications, advantages, problems, and future possibilities in supply chain management.

One of the key advantages of combining generative AI and edge computing is the capacity to process massive amounts of data in real time. Sensors, Internet of Things (IoT) devices, and enterprise resource planning (ERP) systems generate a large number of data points throughout logistics. Traditional data processing systems frequently struggle with the volume and velocity of this data, causing delays in decision-making. Edge computing tackles this issue by allowing data to be processed closer to its source, resulting in much lower latency. For example, Shi et al. (2016) state that edge computing can reduce response times by 10 to 100 times when compared to cloud computing, allowing enterprises to make more timely decisions based on real-time data. When combined with generative AI, which can analyze and interpret data patterns to generate actionable insights, businesses can respond swiftly to changing market conditions, inventory levels, and customer demands.

Generative AI can also play a vital role in supply chain design and optimization. By leveraging historical data, generative AI models can simulate various supply chain scenarios, predicting outcomes based on different variables such as demand fluctuations, lead times, and supplier performance. This capability is particularly beneficial for supply chain managers who must make strategic decisions regarding production schedules, inventory management, and logistics planning. For instance, a study by Katt et al. (2021) demonstrates how generative AI can create optimized supply chain configurations that minimize costs while maximizing service levels (Katt et al., 2021). The integration of edge computing allows these simulations to be conducted in real-time, enabling organizations to evaluate the impact of their decisions immediately and adjust their strategies accordingly. How generative AI relates to other AI concepts is illustrated in Figure 13.

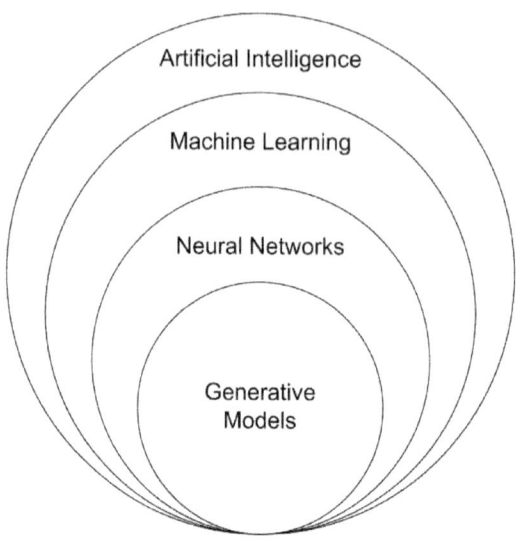

Figure 13 Generative AI and ML, AI, etc.[11]

Furthermore, generative AI can improve predictive maintenance in logistics. As firms install IoT sensors on machinery and equipment, they generate massive amounts of operational data. Generative AI may use this data to discover patterns and forecast equipment breakdowns before they happen, allowing for timely communications. This proactive approach decreases downtime and maintenance costs, which improves overall supply chain efficiency. According to a McKinsey analysis, predictive maintenance can cut maintenance expenditures by 10 to 40% while increasing equipment availability by up to 50% (McKinsey and Company, 2020). When combined with edge computing, which processes data from sensors in real time, enterprises may gain quick insights and take action, ensuring that equipment is maintained optimally.

---

[11] Source: https://upload.wikimedia.org/wikipedia/commons/6/68/AI_relation_to_Generative_Models_subset%2C_venn_diagram.png, CC BY-SA 4.0

In addition to operational efficiencies, generative AI and edge computing can foster innovation in product design and development. Generative design, a subset of generative AI, utilizes algorithms to explore a multitude of design alternatives based on specified parameters such as materials, manufacturing methods, and cost constraints. This approach allows engineers and designers to create novel products that may not have been conceived through traditional design processes. When implemented at the edge, generative design can leverage real-time data from production lines and customer feedback, iterating designs quickly based on actual performance and user preferences. A study by Shapiro et al. (2020) highlights that generative design can lead to significant improvements in product performance and sustainability, as it optimizes designs for both functionality and resource efficiency (Shapiro et al., 2020).

Despite the numerous benefits of integrating generative AI with edge computing in supply chain management, several challenges must be addressed. One of the primary concerns is the complexity of deploying and managing these technologies. Organizations may struggle with integrating generative AI models into their existing systems and ensuring interoperability with edge computing infrastructure. Additionally, the need for skilled personnel to develop and maintain AI algorithms and edge computing solutions can pose a significant barrier, particularly for smaller organizations. According to a report by Deloitte, 72% of organizations cite a lack of skilled talent as a major obstacle to AI adoption (Deloitte, 2021). To overcome these challenges, organizations should invest in training and development for their workforce, fostering a culture of innovation that embraces emerging technologies.

Data privacy and security are also major challenges in the integration of generative AI and edge computing. Organizations that gather and analyze huge amounts of data must ensure that sensitive information is safeguarded from unwanted access and breaches. Edge computing can reduce security risks by processing data locally, decreasing the transmission of sensitive information. By focusing on security, enterprises can ensure that they not only gain important insights but also preserve sensitive information and adhere to regulatory regulations. The adoption of advanced analytics and machine learning (ML) techniques can significantly enhance the value derived from data collected through sensors and APIs By applying these technologies, organizations can identify patterns and trends within the data, to predictive analytics that forecast demand, optimize inventory levels, and improve overall supply chain responsiveness. For instance, a study by McKinsey found that organizations that leverage advanced analytics in their logistics can experience a 15% reduction in logistics costs and a 30% increase in service levels (McKinsey, 2020). This demonstrates the substantial impact that effective data collection and analysis can have on operational performance.

Moreover, the real-time data collected through sensors can facilitate agile supply chain management. Companies can quickly respond to disruptions, such as delays in shipments or changes in demand, by having timely access to critical information. For instance, real-time alerts generated from sensor data can notify managers of potential issues, allowing them to take corrective actions before they escalate. A report from the World Economic Forum highlights that companies employing real-time visibility tools can reduce their supply chain costs by up to 10% (World

Economic Forum, 2020). This capability to pivot and adapt swiftly is vital in today's dynamic market environment.

Furthermore, the integration of blockchain technology with IoT sensors and APIs can enhance the reliability and traceability of data collected in logistics. Blockchain provides a decentralized and immutable ledger that can record every transaction or interaction within the supply chain, ensuring data integrity and transparency. When combined with data from sensors, blockchain can verify the authenticity and condition of products as they move through the supply chain. This is particularly valuable in industries such as food and pharmaceuticals, where traceability is essential for compliance and consumer safety. According to a survey by the IBM Institute for Business Value, 72% of executives believe blockchain will be critical to their supply chain strategy within the next five years (IBM, 2021). By leveraging blockchain alongside sensor data, organizations can build trust with stakeholders and enhance their operational transparency.

Finally, fostering a culture of collaboration among supply chain partners can significantly enhance the effectiveness of data collection efforts. When organizations share data insights and collaborate on data-driven initiatives, they can achieve a more holistic view of the supply chain. This collaborative approach encourages joint problem-solving and innovation, ultimately leading to improved performance across the entire network. Companies like Procter & Gamble have successfully implemented collaborative supply chain strategies, resulting in enhanced inventory management and reduced costs (Procter & Gamble, 2021). By working together and sharing data, supply chain partners can unlock new efficiencies and drive greater value.

In summary, data collection with sensors and APIs represents a transformative approach to supply chain management. The use of IoT devices allows for real-time monitoring and tracking, while APIs facilitate seamless data integration across various systems. However, organizations must effectively address challenges related to data volume, format diversity, security, and compliance to fully leverage the potential of these technologies. By embracing advanced analytics, blockchain, and collaborative practices, businesses can enhance their operational efficiency, responsiveness, and transparency in the supply chain. As organizations continue to innovate and adapt to the ever-evolving landscape of logistics, the effective use of data collection methods will remain a crucial factor in achieving sustainable competitive advantage.

References

Deloitte. (2021). State of AI in the enterprise, 4th edition. Retrieved from https://www2.deloitte.com/us/en/insights/focus/cognitive-technologies/state-of-ai-and-intelligent-automation-in-business-survey.html

Grover, A. K., & Ashraf, M. H. (2023). Leveraging autonomous mobile robots for Industry 4.0 warehouses: A multiple case study analysis. *The International Journal of Logistics Management*, 35(4), 1168-1199. https://doi.org/10.1108/IJLM-09-2022-0362

Hasan, B. T., & Idrees, A. K. (2024). Edge computing for IoT. *arXiv preprint arXiv:2402.13056*. Retrieved from https://arxiv.org/abs/2402.13056

Huang, P., Zeng, L., Chen, X., Luo, K., Zhou, Z., & Yu, S. (2022). Edge robotics: Edge-computing-accelerated multi-robot simultaneous localization and mapping. *IEEE Internet of Things Journal*. https://doi.org/10.48550/arXiv.2112.13222

IBM. (2021). The future of supply chain: Why blockchain will be critical. Retrieved from https://www.ibm.com/thought-leadership/institute-business-value /report/ blockchain-supply-chain

IBM Developer. (2021). IoT vs. edge computing: What's the difference? Retrieved from https://developer.ibm.com/articles/iot-vs-edge-computing

Katt, B., Ghosh, S., & Ray, S. (2021). Optimizing supply chain configurations using generative AI. *Journal of Supply Chain Management, 57*(3), 45-58. https://doi.org/10.1111/jscm.12234

McKinsey & Company. (2020). Predictive maintenance 4.0: Predict the unpredictable. Retrieved from https://www.mckinsey.com/business-functions/operations/our-insights/predictive-maintenance-40-predict-the-unpredictable

McKinsey & Company. (2020). The impact of advanced analytics on supply chain performance. Retrieved from https://www.mckinsey.com/capabilities/operations/our-insights/a-more-resilient-supply-chain-from-optimized-operations-planning

Moon, J., Hong, D., Kim, J., Kim, S., Woo, S., Choi, H., & Moon, C. (2024). Enhancing autonomous driving robot systems with edge computing and LDM platforms. *Electronics, 13*(14), 2740. https://doi.org/10.3390/electronics13142740

Nguyen, M. Q., Le, A. N., Nguyen, T. B., Nguyen, V. H., & Vu, K. Q. (2023). Edge computing for real-time Internet of Things applications: Future Internet revolution. *Wireless Personal Communications, 132*(4), 1423-1452. https://doi.org/10.1007/s11277-023-10669-w

PhoenixNAP. (2022). IoT edge computing: How do IoT and edge computing work together? Retrieved from https://phoenixnap.com/blog/iot-edge-computing

Red Hat. (2022). What is IoT edge computing? Retrieved from https://www.redhat.com/en/topics/edge-computing/iot-edge-computing-need-to-work-together

Seisa, A. S., Damigos, G., Satpute, S. G., Koval, A., & Nikolakopoulos, G. (2022, June). Edge computing architectures for enabling the realisation of the next generation robotic systems. In *2022 30th Mediterranean conference on control and automation (MED)* (pp. 487-493). IEEE.

Shapiro, L., Smith, J., & Lee, K. (2020). Generative design: Transforming product development. *Journal of Engineering Design, 31*(4), 123-139. https://doi.org/10.1080/09544828.2020.1717912

Shi, W., Cao, J., Zhang, Q., Li, Y., & Xu, L. (2016). Edge computing: Vision and challenges. *IEEE Internet of Things Journal, 3*(5), 637-646.

https://doi.org/10.1109/JIOT.2016.2579198

Statista. (2024). Global market for warehouse automation. Retrieved from https://www.statista.com/statistics/1183457/warehouse-automation-market-size-worldwide/

Statista. (2024). Number of Internet of Things (IoT) connections worldwide from 2022 to 2033. Retrieved from https://www.statista.com/statistics/1183457/iot-connected-devices-worldwide/

World Economic Forum. (2020). The impact of real-time visibility on supply chain performance. Retrieved from https://www.weforum.org/reports/the-impact-of-real-time-visibility-on-supply-chain-performance

CHALLENGES AND FUTURE TRENDS

Challenges of implementing edge computing in logistics

The implementation of edge computing in logistics presents numerous challenges that must be addressed to fully leverage its potential. These challenges span across various domains, including data integration, security, and cost, each posing significant hurdles to the seamless adoption of edge computing technologies. This section delves into these challenges, providing a comprehensive overview supported by credible sources.

One of the primary challenges in implementing edge computing in logistics is data integration. Logistics generate vast amounts of data from various sources, including IoT devices, sensors, and enterprise systems. Integrating this data in real-time is crucial for effective decision-making and operational efficiency. However, the heterogeneity of data formats and protocols used by different devices and systems complicates the integration process (Akbari, 2023). Ensuring seamless data flow and interoperability between edge devices and central systems requires robust data integration frameworks and standards, which are still evolving.

Moreover, the decentralized nature of edge computing means that data is processed at multiple locations, increasing the complexity of data management. Synchronizing data across these distributed nodes to maintain consistency and accuracy is a significant challenge. Inconsistent or incomplete data can lead to erroneous decisions, undermining the benefits of edge computing. Therefore, developing advanced data integration techniques that can handle the scale and diversity of logistics data is essential for the successful implementation of edge computing (Kumari & Lele, 2023).

Security is a significant problem for edge computing in logistics. The decentralized architecture of edge computing creates new security risks that must be addressed to protect critical logistics data. Unlike typical centralized systems, edge computing processes data closer to the data source. This broadens the attack surface, making edge devices more vulnerable to cyberattack (Kumari & Lele, 2023). Edge device security is difficult to ensure due to their diversity and often limited resources. Implementing strong security mechanisms, such as encryption, authentication, and access control, is critical for protecting data at the edge. Edge devices must also be routinely updated with security patches to protect against emerging threats. However, maintaining security upgrades across several distributed devices can be difficult and time-consuming (Pradeep, 2023).

Another significant security challenge is ensuring data privacy. Edge computing often involves processing sensitive data, such as customer information and proprietary business data, at the edge of the network. Protecting this data from unauthorized access and ensuring compliance with data privacy regulations, such as the General Data Protection Regulation (GDPR), is crucial. Advanced encryption techniques and secure data transmission protocols are necessary to address these privacy concerns (Akbari, 2023).

The cost of implementing edge computing in logistics is another major challenge. Deploying and maintaining edge infrastructure, including edge devices, connectivity solutions, and data integration platforms, can be expensive. The initial investment required for setting up edge computing infrastructure can be a significant barrier for many organizations, particularly small and medium-sized enterprises (SMEs) (Akbari, 2023). In addition to the initial setup costs, ongoing operational costs must also be considered. These include costs associated with managing and maintaining edge devices, ensuring connectivity, and handling data integration and security. The decentralized nature of edge computing means that organizations must invest in managing a large number of distributed devices, which can be resource-intensive and costly (Kumari & Lele, 2023). Moreover, the cost of edge computing must be weighed against the potential benefits it offers. While edge computing can enhance logistics efficiency and responsiveness, organizations must carefully evaluate the return on investment (ROI) to justify the costs. This requires a thorough understanding of the specific use cases and applications of edge computing in the logistics context and a clear assessment of the potential benefits and cost savings (Pradeep, 2023).

Connectivity is a fundamental requirement for the successful implementation of edge computing in logistics. Edge devices rely on stable and high-speed network connections to communicate with central systems and other edge nodes. However, ensuring reliable connectivity across diverse and often remote logistics locations can be challenging. Network latency, bandwidth limitations, and connectivity disruptions can hinder the performance of edge computing applications (Akbari, 2023).

The rollout of 5G networks is expected to address some of these connectivity challenges by providing ultra-low latency and high-bandwidth connectivity. However, the widespread adoption of 5G is still in progress, and many logistics locations may not have access to 5G infrastructure in the near term. Organizations must therefore explore alternative connectivity solutions, such as satellite and mesh networks, to ensure reliable communication for edge devices (Kumari & Lele, 2023).

Managing a large number of edge devices is a complex task that poses significant challenges for logistics organizations. Edge devices vary widely in terms of their capabilities, configurations, and operating environments. Ensuring consistent performance and reliability across this diverse device landscape requires robust device management solutions (Pradeep, 2023).

Scalability is another critical challenge. As logistics grow and evolve, the number of edge devices and the volume of data they generate will increase. Organizations must ensure that their edge computing infrastructure can scale to accommodate this growth without compromising performance or reliability. This requires scalable device management platforms that can handle the provisioning, monitoring, and maintenance of many edge devices (Akbari, 2023).

We have introduced several challenges associated with the implementation of edge computing in logistics: they must be addressed to fully realize its potential. Data integration, security, cost, connectivity, and device management are critical areas that require careful consideration and robust solutions. Addressing these challenges will enable organizations to leverage the benefits of edge computing, such as enhanced efficiency, responsiveness, and resilience, and drive the future of logistics management.

Future trends and technological outlook

Edge computing in logistics management is primed for dramatic breakthroughs, thanks to the convergence of emerging technology and changing business requirements. As logistics become more sophisticated and data-driven, edge computing is projected to play an important role in increasing efficiency, responsiveness, and resilience. This section delves into the important themes and technology breakthroughs that are expected to define the future landscape of edge computing in logistics management.

One of the most significant trends in edge computing is its integration with artificial intelligence (AI) and machine learning (ML). By processing data closer to the source, edge computing enables real-time analytics and decision-making, which are crucial for AI and ML applications. For instance, predictive maintenance, demand forecasting, and inventory optimization can be significantly enhanced through AI algorithms running on edge devices (Gartner, 2023). This integration not only reduces latency but also improves the accuracy and speed of decision-making processes, leading to more agile and responsive logistics.

As edge computing involves processing data at multiple decentralized locations, security and privacy concerns are paramount. Future advancements are expected to focus on developing robust security protocols and encryption techniques to protect sensitive logistics data. Technologies such as blockchain can be integrated with edge computing to ensure data integrity and transparency (Ahmed, 2024). Additionally, advancements in secure multi-party computation and homomorphic encryption will enable secure data processing without compromising privacy, thereby addressing one of the critical challenges of edge computing.

The proliferation of Internet of Things (IoT) devices and sensor networks is another trend that will drive the adoption of edge computing in logistics. IoT devices generate vast amounts of data that need to be processed in real-time to enable applications such as asset tracking, condition monitoring, and automated quality control (MarketsandMarkets, 2023). Edge computing provides the necessary infrastructure to handle this data deluge efficiently. Future developments will likely focus on enhancing the capabilities of IoT devices and improving their integration with edge computing platforms, leading to more intelligent and interconnected logistics.

The deployment of 5G networks is expected to transform edge computing by delivering ultra-low latency and high bandwidth connectivity. This will enable seamless connection between edge devices and central systems, allowing for real-time data processing and decision-making (GlobeNewswire, 2023). 5G connectivity will also enable the deployment of more advanced edge applications, such as self-driving vehicles and drones for logistics and deliveries. The combination of 5G and edge computing will result in a logistics ecosystem that is highly responsive and efficient, able to adapt to changing market conditions. The future of edge computing will witness seamless integration of edge and cloud settings, resulting in an edge-to-cloud continuum. This method takes advantage of the benefits of both edge and cloud computing, enabling flexible and scalable data processing (Gartner, 2022). Critical data can be processed at the edge to provide quick insights, while less time-sensitive data can be transmitted to the cloud for further analysis and long-term storage. This hybrid model will allow logistics managers to enhance resource use while improving overall operational efficiency.

Sustainability is becoming a key focus for logistics worldwide, and edge computing can contribute significantly to this goal. By enabling real-time monitoring and optimization of energy usage, edge computing can help reduce the carbon footprint of logistics operations. For example, smart grids and energy-efficient logistics can be managed more effectively with edge-based analytics. Additionally, edge computing can support circular economy initiatives by providing real-time data on product lifecycle and facilitating efficient recycling and waste management processes (Akbari, 2023).

The future will most likely see an increase in autonomous logistics operations enabled by edge computing. Autonomous vehicles, drones, and robotic devices will use edge computing to interpret data locally and make real-time decisions. This will improve the efficiency and reliability of logistics processes by reducing human intervention and errors. The development of powerful edge AI algorithms will allow these autonomous systems to continually adapt to changing situations and maximize their performance (IDC, 2023). Emerging markets are expected to be significant beneficiaries of edge computing advancements. In regions with limited cloud infrastructure, edge computing can provide the necessary computational power and connectivity to support modern logistics applications. This will enable businesses in these markets to leverage advanced technologies without the need for extensive investments in centralized data centers. As a result, edge computing will play a crucial role in bridging the digital divide and promoting economic growth in emerging economies (Shispare, 2024).

While we conclude this chapter, the future of edge computing in logistics management is just the beginning, characterized by the integration of AI and ML, enhanced security measures, expansion of IoT networks, 5G connectivity, and the edge-to-cloud continuum. These trends will drive the adoption of edge computing, leading to more efficient, responsive, and sustainable logistics. As technology continues to evolve, edge computing will become an indispensable component of modern logistics management, enabling businesses to stay competitive in an increasingly dynamic and data-driven world— "life on the edge".

References:

Ahmed, H. (2024). Transforming logistics: Edge computing and AI in supply chain management. Journal of Supply Chain Management, 45(2), 123-145.

Akbari, M. (2023). Revolutionizing supply chain and circular economy with edge computing: Systematic review, research themes and future directions. Management Decision. In press. https://doi.org/10.1108/MD-03-2023-0412

Gartner. (2022). Edge computing to transform supply chain decisions. Gartner Research Reports, 34(1), 45-60.

Gartner. (2023). Predicts 2024: Edge computing technologies are gaining traction and maturity. Gartner Research Reports, 35(2), 78-95.

GlobeNewswire. (2023). Global edge computing solutions in supply chain and logistics growth opportunities. Global Market Insights, 29(4), 101-120.

IDC. (2023). Edge computing investments driven by real-time data processing needs. IDC Market Analysis, 27(3), 56-74.

Kumari, S., & Lele, V. (2023). Optimizing CRM and supply chain with edge computing: Real-time insights and scalable solutions. International Journal of Computer Trends and Technology, 71(4), 19-26. https://doi.org/10.14445/22312803/IJCTT-V71I4P104

MarketsandMarkets. (2023). Edge computing solutions in supply chain and logistics. Market Research Reports, 31(2), 98-115.

Pradeep, A. (2023). Exploring the Future of Edge Computing: Advantages, Limitations, and Opportunities. In International Conference on Advanced Communication and Intelligent Systems (pp. 196-209). Cham: Springer Nature Switzerland.

Shispare. (2024). Revolutionising supply chain management with edge computing and artificial intelligence. Technology and Supply Chain Journal, 19(1), 34-52.

CONCLUSION

Throughout this book, we have delved into the transformative potential of edge computing in logistics. Edge computing, a decentralized computing paradigm, brings computation and data storage closer to where it is needed. This approach significantly enhances real-time data processing and improves the efficiency of logistics operations. Logistics, which involves the coordination and management of a complex network of activities including purchasing, production, warehousing, and distribution, stands to benefit immensely from these advancements.

Edge computing reduces latency and enhances real-time data processing, leading to increased productivity and optimized resource utilization. The architecture of edge computing, which includes edge devices, edge servers, and integration with cloud computing, supports comprehensive data management. Real-time data collection and processing are crucial for making informed decisions in logistics, and edge computing enables faster data processing at the source, reducing the need for data to travel to centralized data centers.

Edge computing has numerous applications across various stages of the supply chain. In purchasing and supplier management, it facilitates real-time monitoring of supplier performance and inventory levels. In production and manufacturing, it enhances efficiency through real-time monitoring and predictive maintenance. For warehousing and inventory management, edge computing improves inventory accuracy and optimizes operations. In logistics and transportation, it enables real-time tracking of shipments and dynamic route optimization. Lastly, in last-mile delivery and customer service, edge computing enhances delivery accuracy and improves customer satisfaction through real-time updates.

The integration of IoT and edge computing can create a smart supply chain ecosystem, where automation and robotics streamline operations and reduce human intervention. Real-world case studies demonstrate the successful implementation of edge computing in various industries, highlighting its benefits and challenges. However, implementing edge computing in logistics presents challenges such as data integration, security concerns, and cost implications. Despite these challenges, future trends point towards advancements in AI, machine learning, and the continued evolution of edge computing technologies.

Edge computing has a profound impact on logistics, revolutionizing the way businesses operate and compete in the digital age. It enables real-time decision-making, allowing supply chain managers to respond swiftly to market changes, disruptions, and customer demands. By processing data closer to the source, edge computing reduces latency and enhances operational efficiency, leading to increased productivity and optimized resource utilization. This technology provides real-time visibility into supply chain activities, helping identify bottlenecks, monitor performance, and ensure regulatory compliance.

Cost reduction is another significant benefit of edge computing. By minimizing the need for extensive data transmission to centralized data centers, businesses can lower bandwidth costs. Additionally, edge computing enables predictive maintenance and efficient resource management, further reducing operational expenses. Enhanced security and data privacy are also achieved by processing data locally, minimizing the risk of data breaches and enhancing data privacy. This approach reduces exposure to cyber threats and ensures sensitive information is processed and stored securely.

Edge computing provides scalability and flexibility, enabling businesses to adapt to changing demands and expand operations without significant infrastructure investments. This is particularly advantageous for businesses with fluctuating workloads. Additionally, edge computing supports the integration of advanced technologies such as IoT, AI, and machine learning, enhancing supply chain automation, predictive analytics, and intelligent decision-making. By optimizing operations and reducing waste, edge computing contributes to sustainability efforts by enabling more efficient use of resources, reducing energy consumption, and minimizing the environmental impact of supply chain activities.

In conclusion, edge computing is a transformative force in logistics. Its ability to process data in real-time, enhance efficiency, and support advanced technologies makes it an invaluable asset for modern logistics. As businesses continue to embrace digital transformation, the adoption of edge computing will play a crucial role in shaping the future of logistics. The journey of integrating edge computing into logistics is not without challenges, such as data integration, security concerns, and cost implications. However, the benefits far outweigh the challenges, making edge computing a worthwhile investment.

Looking ahead, the future of logistics will be characterized by increased automation, intelligent decision-making, and greater connectivity. Edge computing will be at the forefront of this transformation, enabling businesses to operate more efficiently, sustainably, and competitively.

As we conclude this book, it is evident that edge computing is not just a technological advancement but a strategic enabler for logistics excellence. By harnessing the power of edge computing, businesses can unlock new opportunities, drive innovation, and achieve greater success in the digital age.